THE RUNAWAY GAME

By Stephen J Feins

Other Books by Stephen J. Feins (sjfeins.com)

- Mystery
    - The Invisible Assassin
    - The Pine Meadow Hunt
    - The Riverbed
    - Objective: POTUS
    - Revenge: The Many Suspects
    - The Sacred Foot Murders
    - The Case of the Twisted Judgement
    - The Case of One Too Many
    - Project Spider
- Fiction
    - Traci
    - The Flow
    - The Route 17 Bus
    - The Last god
    - Sabotage of a Noble Cause
    - The Odyssey of the U-996
    - Double Danger
    - The Eighth Step
    - The Million Dollar Investigation
    - Who Is Jason Foster?
    - Brains Enough
    - A Gauge to Glory
    - Two Steps Forward
    - George Washington, Defendant
    - Stein's Odyssey
- Crime and Justice
    - Twelve Honest Women
    - The Trial: A Russian Riddle
    - RV Justice: Misfits with Badges
    - The Illusion of Cutter Bay
- Romance
    - The Next Chapter: What The Heart Wants
    - Love's Scary Dilemma
- Science Fiction
    - Gamble at Point Zero
    - Battle of the Dark Star
    - Potten's Folly: Earth
    - The Thaxsis Protocol

Dedication

To my readers who enjoy my books and then became part of my very nice following. I hope my future books bring as much pleasure as my previous ones did. Thank you for your support.

The accounts and descriptions in this work are fictional, and any resemblance to any person, living or dead, is purely coincidental. All places used in this work are approximations of actual locations. Any use of any part of this work is prohibited without the consent of the author except in the case of legitimate critical review.

Copyright - ©Stephen J. Feins, April 8, 2024

Chapter One

And so it came to pass: the lightning, the thunder, the wind, and the rain. And it continued for six months without a break or a let p. The oceans swelled to overtake the land and wash away homes like pebbles on a beach. What was needed is someone who has the skills to rebuild after the total destruction of the land masses. Now most of mankind wandered from place to place seeking shelter, food, and water. It would take a charismatic individual to save the world…

"Marvin, turn off that game and come set the table."

It took three times for Marvin to acknowledge the demand. He pressed pause and hid the controller to be sure no one touched it. The game was brand new and because of his status as 'Beta Tester' he was anxious to get back to it. He was paid two hundred dollars to edit games.

The Foster family lived in a ranch style home about two miles north of the Canadian / U. S. border. There were six other homes on the street with the Fosters living at the end of the cul-de-sac. The neighborhood was quite new with a mix of many cultures. Marvin, sixteen, was one of many teenagers who lived there. His sister, Mary, eighteen, was about to leave for college. His parents, Claire, a librarian and John, a contractor who built the house, had been married for twenty years and were looking forward to an anniversary cruise to Bermuda.

"Marvin, sweetheart, how many times do I have to tell you the forks go on the left side of the plate."

"Sorry, mom. Maybe I shouldn't help set the table since I get everything wrong."

"Maybe you should stop playing those games and use the time to practice setting the table."

Mary came into the dining room and smiled. "Pain, (she used her pet name for him), with me leaving you are going to have to step up and take over all the chores in the house."

"Don't worry Pin Head, (his nickname for her), I can handle it with far less complaining than you do."

Claire had had enough. "Okay, you two sit down and stop the bickering. Your father will be late so we will have dinner without him."

Just as they sat down there was a knock on their door. They were not expecting anyone so Marvin cautiously opened the door, peeking out. Standing there were three of the biggest soldiers he had ever seen. They wore service dress uniforms with one being a General who was very thin and with his bald head he looked like a pencil. His appearance caused Marvin to smile. The other two were Captains and they were built like rugby players. Marvin backed away from the door.

"Mom, you better come here. Quick!"

Claire approached the men. "Is there something wrong? What are you doing here?"

The General looked at Marvin. "We are sorry to come without calling but there is a high-level emergency. We need to take your son to our Command Central."

Claire started to panic. "What? I want you to take the others and leave. NOW!"

The General shook his head. "I am terribly sorry but we need Marvin's help. There are hundreds of thousands of lives at risk. I promise no harm will come to him. If you like you can come with us. But Marvin will be going with us."

Just then a Royal Canadian Police car arrived with lights flashing. Two police officers walked up. "I am Sergeant Guy Morissette. We got a call from someone in this house about an emergency. What is going on here?"

Claire stepped forward. "These men are trying to kidnap my son!"

The General turned toward the police. "Sergeant Morissette, I am General George Campbell from Unified Command in Quebec. This involves state security. Let me talk with your supervisor."

The Sergeant handed the General his radio. "That would be Superintendent Lavoie."

"Superintendent Lavoie, this is General Campbell."

The General walked some distance away while talking. He returned and handed the radio to the policeman. After a short conversation, the police nodded. "I'm sorry, I have been informed that this action has been approved at the very highest level."

The police returned to their car and left the scene. The General then addressed Claire. "I wish I could tell you more but we really have to take Marvin with us. Please pack a bag for him and if you have decided to come with us, please get ready. You will be gone for several days."

Claire was in tears and Mary came out to steady her. "If any harm comes to my brother…"

"Captain Sprague will go with your brother to pack. Please know that your country takes this very seriously and will do everything in our power to protect Marvin."

Claire looked at Mary. "I have to stay here to fill in your father."

Fifteen minutes later the military and Marvin left the house that Marvin had grown up in. He was not sure he would ever see it again.

Chapter Two

Marvin Robert Foster was a product of the twenty-first century. He was playing on a computer at age three and by age five he had written his first little game. From there his parents put him in a programming club at school and by age ten he was the leader of the club having written four sophisticated games. He was tested by the school department and moved to a special 'gifted and talented' high school at age eleven.

Marvin was now a teenager standing six feet tall with broad shoulders, dark black hair, brown eyes, round face, and a protruding stomach from sitting in front of a computer getting little exercise. With support from his parents, Marvin designed a computer workroom which his father constructed in their home. He entered all types of competitions and took first prize in many of them. 'SkyDreams', a computer games maker, was very impressed with his skills and offered him a job as 'Beta Tester' for their new games. In a short time he was testing and editing games.

At this time he was editing a new game called 'World Obliteration'. It centered around a maniacal genius who had decided only he could save the earth. The script read that the mad man was trying to cleanse the earth of its wars, hatred, greed, pollution, and political divisions that were destroying the planet. The game featured levels of destruction where the player had to use various tools to stop the ruthless leader from destroying some part of the world. The graphics were frightfully beyond even his skills.

Marvin never met the author of the game but was totally blown away by the beauty of the code. He edited characters and how tools would work against the mad man. He added a couple of new challenges and the carnage was up a level. He could tell the game would be a massive hit and he would receive five percent of the net profit.

His work sounded as if he was just playing games and his parents wanted everyone to know just how talented he was. They would brag about Marvin and were interviewed several times by newspapers and magazines. Claire and John became minor celebrities but in the back of their minds they were worried about Marvin's social development. He had only one friend and he seemed to have no interest in girls or dating. They made sure he went to an exercise program to get him away from the computer for a little while and help keep him healthy.

They arrived at Command Central. Marvin sat in a small room that looked like a renovated telephone booth. There was one small table with four chairs, two on each side. The walls were painted in a gray color and there was one window at the top of the wall over the door. The floor was cement. There was a camera mounted on the wall across from him.

The door opened and General Campbell came in along with a civilian. "Marvin, I know you must have a hundred questions but I would ask you to wait until Mr. Faulkner finishes his presentation."

Marvin leaned forward. "You kidnapped me at dinner time and I am starving. Also, I'm not sure you have the authority to hold me unless I have committed a crime. Don't I get my rights? How about that phone call?"

Campbell raised his hand. "Easy, Marvin. We mean you no harm. Please listen to Mr. Faulkner. He will answer all your questions. I have sent out for pizza."

Marvin smiled. "With peppers and onions, I hope!"

Faulkner opened his briefcase and placed photos on the small table. Marvin looked at them and was appalled. They were pictures of what looked like a village that had been struck by an earthquake and a tsunami. There were dead bodies floating in the water, some of whom were children.

The stranger introduced himself. "My name is Ronald Faulkner and I am now working with the United States Department of Homeland Security. These photos were taken recently in a small village on the island of Guam. As you can see there are no buildings standing and the fields have been burnt. The death toll right now is one hundred and ten with another three hundred injured."

Marvin had trouble keeping his composure. "Why are you showing me these photos? What have I got to do with it? I want to go home."

Faulkner continued. "I'm showing you the photos is we believe you can stop this from happening. We need you to work with us to prevent a very dangerous man from doing this again."

Marvin shook his head. "I have no idea what you are talking about."

The General took out an 'eyes only' file. "The destruction of Guam fits the exact pattern of destruction laid out in the game you have been working on. We believe this game caused this destruction although we do not know how it did so.

Since you worked on the program, we believe you can turn it off."

The teen sat with a painful look. "But I didn't create the game. It was created by 'E1brad6L'. He is the one who can stop the game from running."

"That's the problem. We do not know who this 'E1brad6L' is or where he is. We contacted the company, 'SkyDreams', and they claim they only communicated over the computer. The game appears to have been invented by this E1brad6L freelancer who was trying to break into the computer game business."

Marvin slumped in his chair. "Why do you need me?"

Faulkner continued. "The program contains a security system we have never seen before. That's where you come in. Since you worked on the program you must know about security."

Marvin pushed the photos away. "If the guy who created the game put in special security level codes, then I am not sure I can help. You must have very talented guys who can break the code."

Campbell spoke up. "We have already tried but the security code is so unusual we cannot hack it. I would love to have this guy on our side in our cyber wars. When you worked on the program you had to temporarily shut off the security codes. We are hoping you can do that again."

Marvin nodded. "Yes and the security code is simple. It is FV12S."

Campbell called over to his aide. "Roger, try this code!"

While they waited, Marvin's thoughts turned to Guam. "I'm still not sure how the program destroyed that village."

Roger reported back. "Sorry General, the code does not work."

Faulkner again tried to answer Marvin's questions. "We believe the program is following its written narrative.

"*'My name is Resurrection. I am the only one who can cleanse the planet. I and I alone know what must be done. Try and stop me if you can. I have developed a special weapon that combines a sonic heat wave with a sound vibration protocol supported by bright light that blinds. You have only forty-eight hours to stop me. Good Luck!'*"

"Okay, yes, I wrote that passage but there is no such thing as a sonic heat wave weapon that causes sound vibrations which would destroy life. It is pure fantasy."

Campbell shook his head. "Someone invented that machine and it operates exactly as it does in the game. "

"But since my code does not work, there is very little I can do to help you."

Campbell raised a new issue. "Why did the machine attack a village on Guam? There seems to be no reason."

Marvin shrugged his shoulders. "That's on me. When I edited the game I had to put in coordinates and locations to satisfy the machine's operating system. I gave the machine the coordinates of a village I saw on National Geographic."

Faulker became highly animated. "So all the other chapters have some real-world location?"

"Yes."

Faulker picked up his cell. "We can fortify or abandon areas in the games matrix and slow it down. Put me through to the Canadian Prime Minister."

"Prime Minister, we have Marvin, the beta tester, but unfortunately even his code does not work. It appears the next target is in the United States. General Campbell has set up a command center in Maine just across the border. We can work from there and I can keep in touch with the American President."

Chapter Three

The search for the game developer, 'E1brad6L' now took on more of an urgency. With Marvin's code not working, a call was sent out for volunteer hackers who might be able to break into the game code. Marvin and the others left the small room to ride in a waiting helicopter. The trip was only ten minutes and they landed at what looked like an old airfield. They headed to a hangar and once inside Marvin was blown away at what he saw.

On both sides were banks and banks of computers and servers. Men and women were working either alone or in tandem. The back wall was a communication hub with radios and landlines connecting it to countries around the world. The center was filled with cafeteria-type serving and a stand-alone kitchen to prepare food. There were no windows, but the climate control kept the area comfortable.

Marvin was taken over to one of the computer stations. "General Campbell…"

"Call me George."

"I don't think I can do that but I'll try. I don't understand why you just don't destroy the game and the code."

A woman joined the station. "Because the program was written by AI and it has taken over the security function."

Marvin shook his head. "That's not good."

"The game is housed in the cloud and if we cannot shut it off, our failsafe plan is to destroy everything in the cloud. That would mean everything anyone saved to the cloud will be gone. We would have to recreate every bit of information. That's why it is a last resort."

Campbell added the last piece. "AI has taken over the cloud and the program is drawing power much like how Bluetooth operates. It is also taking radio and television waves and transferring them into power."

Marvin just sat quietly trying to remember the code he put into the program. Perhaps if they found that it would be a way to shut it down. He got up and took Campbell over to a large screen where the text of the game was displayed. "If we read the chapter-by-chapter text we can determine where the next strike will be. Chapter one was a village that I based on Guam's location. Chapter two is an airport based on the layout of Chicago's O'Hare. And chapter three is based in Japan."

The General made a quick exit and headed for the communication center where he placed a call to the President. "Mr. President, we need to evacuate and shut down O'Hare airport. I have reason to believe it will be the next area to be hit."

While the General was on the phone, Marvin was joined by the strange woman who had approached him earlier. She was approximately forty or so and stood with shoulders back. Her face had no makeup and did not need any. Her hair was prematurely white. She was dressed in overalls which did not take detract, but rather enhanced a very attractive woman. "Marvin, my name is Madeline Kraus, I am…"

"Miss Kraus, there is no need for you to introduce yourself. You are the dean of 'Hackers Anonymous' and have traced many 'black hats' over the years. I have admired your work and have read everything you have written."

"Thank you for that. And you are quite famous yourself. I think if we cannot stop this thing, no one can. What do you know about E1brad6L?"

"Not much, I'm afraid. He contacted me right after my last game hit the market. He said he was impressed by the coding and had a game he needed to be edited. He offered five thousand dollars and a percentage of sales. I would have done it for free but I didn't tell him that."

Kraus was taking notes. "Did you ever meet him? Talk with him? See him?"

"The sad answer is no. He was very private and whenever we texted it was always about the game. I tried asking general questions but he never answered. As far as I know he is a recluse with a brilliant mind."

"So there are no clues we can use to try and find him."

Marvin nodded. "The only thing I can think of is his mention of his lab with its view of the Florida Keys."

"That gives us something to work with. I will give the information to Faulkner and he and his men can work on it."

"Who is this Faulkner? He said he is attached to Homeland Security."

"He works for one of those agencies with only three letters in its name."

Suddenly a loud alarm went off. Everyone gathered around the main screen which practically filled up the whole front wall. Scenes of O'Hare flashed on the screen displaying rain and wind that surpassed hurricane conditions. The terminal buildings began to shake and collapse. The roadways buckled and cracked. Planes were dissolving and leaving puddles of metal. It was an eerie scene straight out of one of those B disaster movies.

And then it was over. Not a building or hangar remained standing. At least twelve aircraft had melted. There was not a road that led into the airport that was passable. The only saving grace was the President's order to abandon the airport. There were no deaths, but almost ninety people suffered burns and injuries.

Faulkner walked over to Marvin and Kraus. "We need to find E1brad6L before the next chapter in the book. What is it?"

Marvin pointed to the chapter display scene. "The next target will be a cruise ship and its port. I will have to get my notes to remind me of which port I used."

The race to stay ahead of the program was now paramount. Only the search for E1brad6L was more important.

Chapter Four

Other countries were now aware of the threat. Special links were created so experts six thousand miles away could contribute as if they were in the same room. Kraus continued to work on finding the key to the security lockout. Marvin looked for the back door he had inserted. Neither was having much luck.

"Miss Kraus…"

"Marvin, I appreciate the social context but please call me Madeline. Or better still, Maddy."

"Maddy, I checked on some code that made no sense. I have no idea why it is even here. See if this makes sense to you."

She looked over the code and then entered it into the program. The computer seemed to ignore it and she thought it was another dead end. "Sorry, Marvin but this goes nowhere."

Marvin thought for a moment. "Why would he put code into the program if it didn't do anything?"

"We would have to ask E1brad6L."

Marvin suddenly jumped up and ran over to the central computer. He ran the lines of code and stopped. The piece of code that did nothing was in the security pathway. "That's it! Now I know why we can't stop the program."

Campbell heard Marvin and, along with several others, joined him. "What did you find?"

Marvin pushed the ESC key. "The reason we cannot find the key to unlock the program is due to the fact it needs TWO keys, not just one. I remember talking with E1brad6L about our favorite movies. We both loved the conflict between two military officers about arming a nuclear missile."

Campbell shook his head. "I don't understand what you are getting at."

"Okay. In all the movies it takes two keys, inserted, and turned at exactly the same time, to arm and launch the missile. We need to have two codes or keys, enter them at the same time, and press one of the keys on the keyboard."

Kraus smiled. "That makes sense. What you have is one of the keys. We need to find the second code and which key we have to press. I'm afraid the only way to do that is to find E1brad6L and persuade him to help us."

Faulkner joined the discussion. "I have gone through all my NSA programs and I cannot find any trace of this E1brad6L person. He is off the grid. I went through Marvin's bank records to try and trace E1brad6L's payment to Marvin. The money was paid in cash so there is no visible record."

Marvin quickly pulled up his bank statements. There was no deposit of the money. "I know I saw it. It came in four months ago…wait a minute, something is missing. My backup listing says I had four deposits but the screen only shows three. E1brad6L has erased the payment record."

Faulkner rushed back to his computer. "Nothing is ever gone permanently from the computer's clutches. We now have an important clue to finding this guy."

Marvin was busy trying to identify the cruise ship and port he used in the program when his sister called on his cell. "Hi Sis, what's the problem?"

"Dad had a fall while working on a project. He is in Saint Vincent's Hospital and is going into surgery. Mom is there and I know we should both be there."

"How bad is it?"

"The doctors don't know. He is bleeding internally and has at least two broken ribs. I'm scared. He might not…"

"Mary, calm down. We have the best medical care in the world."

Mary's voice was filled with fear. "Can you pick me up on the way to the hospital?"

Marvin was conflicted. He wanted to be with his family but there was a third target about to be destroyed with the loss of many lives. "I can't get away now. I will join you just as soon as I can."

Mary was more insistent. "He's your father! We need to be there. Mom has gone to pieces with worry. Your family is your most important need!"

Kraus walked over and heard the conversation. "Marvin, go. We will find the target and warn the people."

Marvin was now close to yelling in frustration. "HOW? I have to find the ship and port I put into the program. A cruise ship holds thousands of passengers and crew!"

"Take your notes with you and work while you wait at the hospital."

Marvin was close to tears. "What am I going to do? I cannot live with the deaths of all those people and I cannot live with not being there should my father die!"

Campbell heard the loud discussion. "Give us your notes and we will figure it out. Now go!"

Marvin was now frozen in his chair, unable to move or make up his mind.

Chapter Five

Madeline Kraus (Maddy) grew up in a time when women were able to pursue any career they wished. Companies that were mostly male now worked for a balance of men and women. There were more female CEOs and government leaders. There were special laws protecting women in schools from discrimination. Women were making inroads everywhere except in one key place, the family. Parents still pushed for the 'old days' where women could work but needed to find a man and have children.

In Maddy's case, her father wanted her to go to an all-girls college near her home in Toronto. Her major would be in Liberal Arts and prepare her for working with people in hospitals or schools. Her father said it was a waste for her to study math and science, so that is exactly what she did. Her father cut off funding for college when Maddy was accepted at MIT. Fortunately, she received a full scholarship and stayed to earn a Ph.D. and taught undergraduates in computer science courses.

At age thirty she was approached by a joint United States and Canada operation under the direction of U. S. Homeland Security. Her job was to work with others in cybersecurity and locate hackers. Her first case involved an attack on a small water treatment plant outside of Toronto. The hackers wanted money to unfreeze the plant. Maddy found the culprits in less than two hours. Police raided the home and arrested two individuals. She was on her way to establishing herself as the dean of 'black hats'.

She was placed on loan and travelled a lot in the last ten years. There were opportunities for romance but her schedule cut every relationship short. Just when she found someone, she would be sent off to another city or country and disappear for weeks. Finally, she gave up and accepted the single life. Her record of accomplishments continued to soar and now, at the age of thirty-six, she became the head of the cybersecurity team and was on loan to General Campbell.

An ambulance took Marvin to the hospital where he met his mother and sister. His father was still in surgery and the injury report was a lot better. His ribs had not been broken, only bruised, and the internal bleeding had been repaired. However, during the operation the doctors found a mass, a tumor, attached to his spine. They were preparing to remove it and test it for cancer. Marvin needed to busy his mind so he went to work in the hospital cafeteria.

His sister Mary joined him at the table. "So brother dear, it looks like things are better than when I first informed you of dad's fall."

"I am happy for that. Now I need to find a location that might be the next victim."

Mary looked puzzled. "Next victim of what?"

He had to be careful about what he said. The work was top secret. "Say, Mary, do you remember my working on a project and I got so frustrated I needed something to relax? I could use that now."

"I don't think they will let you play those Japanese cartoons in the hospital."

Marvin raised his head. "What Japanese cartoons?"

"There was a time when you watched those things all day long. You were so taken by Japan I thought you were going to take a cruise there. You were looking at this huge boat…"

Marvin stood straight up causing the papers in front of him to fly all over. "Mary, this is important, do you remember anything about the ship?"

She picked up his pages and leafed through them. She pulled out a page with numbers and coordinates on it. "See for yourself."

Marvin remembered. "I was looking at the Imabari Shipbuilding Group that was building the largest cruise ship in the world. It would be docked at Kure where the Yamato Museum is located."

Marvin ran out of the cafeteria and to the hospital's communication area. "This is an emergency. Life or Death. I need to use your landline!"

The nurse looked very surprised and due to the urgency Marvin demonstrated, she turned over the phone to him. He called the group. "Let me speak to Maddy. **And hurry!**"

"This is Maddy. Is that you Marvin? How is your dad?"

Marvin was out of breath. "Maddy, I found the target. It will be the port of Imabari in Japan. They are building what will be the largest cruise ship in the world."

"That's great, Marvin! We will get a warning out immediately!"

The news was also good about John Foster, Marvin's dad. The tumor was benign and although he would be in some pain for a while he should make a full recovery. Mother, daughter, and son hugged and there were plenty of happy tears.

Maddy informed the General and Faulkner who then contacted their Japanese counterparts. "George, thanks for the warning. Unfortunately, the CEO of Imabari is on board the ship in drydock. I am talking with the Japanese most senior official, Haruto. He says the CEO is refusing to believe what we told him. He is blocking the evacuation of the shipyard. We have people on the way. How much time do we have?"

Campbell looked at Faulkner. "What do I tell him? We have no idea on the timing."

Faulkner took the phone. "Haruto, you have to get the people out of there. We have a belief it will be in the next couple of hours."

Campbell covered the mouthpiece of the phone with his hand. "Ronald, you have no proof of that!"

"General, I'd rather apologize later than attend hundreds of funerals."

Chapter Six

Kaito Agawa was the director of the shipbuilding project creating the largest cruise ship ever to go to sea. The yard was filled with hundreds of workers each with a specific part of the ship to finish. With Royal Caribbean's 'Icon of The Seas' already having been launched, Agawa and his investors were in a hurry to surpass that ship. While the 'Icon of The Seas' was 1,198 feet long with twenty decks and could accommodate seven thousand, six hundred passengers, the 'Rising Sun' would be 1,545 feet with twenty-five decks and accommodate nine thousand passengers.

And the 'Rising Sun', along with the pride Japan could bask in, would cater to a special Japanese guest list of prominent political leaders, famous athletes, and media stars. There would be several outdoor areas reflecting Japan's past and they would be decorated with works by Japanese artists. The cost of the ship was just shy of three billion dollars and an interior stateroom would cost two thousand, five hundred dollars per person.

Japanese tourists made up a large number of cruise passengers, and other cruise ship companies were planning to make it difficult for the 'Rising Sun' to dock in other ports. Already Miami was expanding its docking area for the larger ships. Agawa had overseen the project since it began some three years ago. The workers were loyal to him and followed his orders without question. That is why he had to be convinced to evacuate and tell his workers to do also.

Haruto Sato, Deputy Director of the Japanese Ministry of Shipping and Commerce, had now been told by Faulkner about the two-hour window the shipyard had. He met with Ryan Masters from the U.S. Embassy staff and they headed off to Kure. When they got there the shipyard was in full operation. They had to get to Agawa and convince him to abandon the entire port.

Agawa was in his office which was located on the top deck of the 'Rising Sun'. Haruto entered first. "Agawa-san, why haven't you closed the yard and evacuated? There is little time left."

"Who is this person with you?"

"He is Ryan Masters from the U. S. Embassy. He is here to help with the evacuation. He has knowledge of the threat."

Agawa looked at Masters. "Are you CIA or one of those other groups?"

Masters bowed. "Agawa-san, the danger is very real. We have already seen the destruction of this force on Guam and O'Hare Airport. Please help us save your men and this great ship."

Agawa was standing next to the bridge controls and occasionally would rub his hand on them. "Perhaps you are from Royal Caribbean and are trying to embarrass me. If I shut down, I will be the laughingstock of the industry."

Masters tried again. "Please, believe me, we are not trying to trick you into making a bad decision."

Suddenly the ship began to shake, just a little. The temperature in the ship was rising steadily and several workers had to grab on for fear of falling. "You see, it is starting!"

Agawa shook his head. "That is only the land giving way to earth tremors. We have them all the time."

The temperature continued to rise. The bridge thermometer recorded one hundred and two. The ship began to shake so badly that it moved off of one of the steel arms holding it in drydock. Haruto began to raise his voice. "Kaito, you must act now. The attack is happening now!"

Masters reached for the microphone on the bridge and broadcast, in his finest Japanese, for the workers to abandon the yard. But the workers would not move. They were waiting for Agawa. Meanwhile the shaking and heat continued.

Masters turned to Haruto. "I'm sorry. We have to get out of here, now!"

Agawa finally got on the microphone and began to tell the men to evacuate, but it was too late. The steel framework became soft and returned to its molten stage. Deck after deck collapsed upon itself until there were no upper deck structures. They could hear the men screaming. The top floor was still intact but signs of it breaking up were everywhere. Masters took a running start and jumped off the bridge onto the landing. Unfortunately, the landing was collapsing and Masters fell hundreds of feet into the docking bay.

The destruction was devastating. Men were crushed under soft steel pieces and many men were set ablaze. In the confusion and panic, workers crowded in doorways blocking the path out. Roof portions collapsed burying many. Suddenly the ship exploded with rivets being sent out like bullets. Many fell as if they had been shot. The bridge was gone as were its occupants. Emergency vehicles had to stay far back for fear of being enveloped in the destruction. Several first responders were hit with flying shrapnel rivets. The death toll began to rise quickly.

Faulkner and Campbell could only listen to the sounds of the disaster. A helicopter finally arrived at the scene and sent back the first pictures. The entire yard was awash in flames and the sea gate that kept the ocean out of the drydock gave way. Water rushed in doing even more damage. The heat created large steam clouds blocking some of the video from the helicopter. No one in the Command Center could watch for long. They may not have known the workers but they felt their pain and suffering.

Campbell tried to connect with someone. "Masters…Haruto…anyone. What is happening? Is there any hope of people surviving?"

The line went dead. It was too late to do anything. The game 'World Obliteration' had just finished its third chapter. Faulkner screamed and threw a chair into one of the monitor screens. It would be days before at least some accounting was released. Ryan Masters, Haruto Sato, Kaito Agawa and over two hundred men were killed. The fires were still burning despite the efforts of the Japanese emergency services.

Faulkner turned to Campbell. "**WE MUST FIND E1brad6L NOW!!**"

Chapter Seven

People bond for all sorts of reasons. Some are part of an athletic team, some share the same ideas, some belong to a book club, but in this case it was a bond formed by the three disasters that took the lives of hundreds of people. Marvin, being sixteen, took the losses the hardest. The team sat at the conference table in the Command Center and barely spoke a word. Somehow they must stop the game from causing more deaths and destruction.

"Marvin, how is your dad?"

Marvin almost did not hear the question. "He is better. The ribs were just bruised and the bleeding was not as bad as it looked. He will be home soon."

Faulkner looked up. "So, Marvin, how is your father?"

It went like that for most of the morning. Marvin took out every bit of correspondence he had with E1brad6L. On one of the first emails he noticed a picture he sent of the beautiful beach he was writing from. It was his private cave where he could work and not be bothered. What caught Marvin's eye was the small billboard in the corner of the photo.

"Mr. Faulkner…"

"Ronald."

"Ronald, I have blown up this picture E1brad6L sent me. I can read some words on this billboard. It says '… *your KEY LA…*' "

"What are you getting at?"

Marvin was getting excited. "The man said he could write all day while looking out at the warm sand and beautiful ocean. He was in a cove or cave away from any distraction. This says to me warm climate, beautiful sand, and caves where water washes in and out. That kind of an area would have to be a place tourists go for vacation."

Campbell was scribbling on some paper and had written down the three words Marvin had found. "You know, it sounds like the Keys."

Faulkner looked at the drawings. "Yes, it could be the Keys, the Florida Keys."

Kraus opened her laptop and googled the Florida Keys. "There are islands someone could be lost on if they wanted to be alone. We need to do a search of the Keys that have off the grid areas."

The entire team was energized. Campbell sent out an alert and had every soldier and sailor combing the island chain. It was a long shot but at least they were doing something. Kraus looked at maps of the Keys. "We should contact realtors. Our guy probably bought a house near the beach as his primary residence. He then could spend as much time as he wanted on the beach in his 'cave'."

Two days later and with no sign of an area which fit the parameters, Marvin came rushing in. "I contacted the game company and got their emails. I figured he must be near somewhere he could get food and where he could find entertainment. The emails they sent me had the same sign but more of it."

Faulkner took the email picture and put it next to the email picture they had been working with. "That's it!!? There is part of a word. It says '…GO vacation dream…'"

The team looked at the two pieces trying to combine them. "…your 'KEY LA…' and 'GO vacation dream…'. Kraus took a marker, went to the board, and entered the letter 'R'. And there it was "…your KEY LARGO vacation dream…'.

Campbell ran over to the communications area and broadcast a search pattern for Key Largo.

Again it took two days before they had their answer. There were five people on the beach with a house close by. E1brad6L had to be one of them. The vetting process began with one eye on what might be the next target.

General Campbell offered a course of action. "Okay people let's try and winnow down the list. All the persons of interest live on Fleming Key. One person is transient and only spends a few weeks in Florida. One person is a sixteen-year-old girl living with her parents. And one person is recovering from surgery on his hands and arms that were burned in a fire some four months ago. That leaves us with only two suspects. I suggest we all head to the Fleming Key and interview the last two suspects. Marvin can go with us as he has had dealings with E1brad6L in the past and there might be something brought up in conversation that will tip Marvin off."

An American Air Force jet was pressed into service and the team got on board. Campbell, Kraus, Faulkner, and Marvin, along with special forces soldiers, left for Miami. It was a long flight which gave Marvin time to figure out what might be the fourth target.

Faulkner was seated beside Kraus. "I don't know about you, but I am exhausted. I have trouble sleeping and work is piling up at my office."

"I know how you feel. I have fitful sleep and by the time the alarm goes off I have gotten about three hours of sleep."

He watched her yawn which set off his own yawn. "You know, this will be a long flight. Why not stretch out and take a nap. It will do you a world of good. I will wake you if anything important happens."

"Mr. Faulkner…"

"Please, call me Ron…"

"Ron, I will take you up on that. I just hope I don't snore and embarrass myself."

"I don't believe that is possible."

Kraus grabbed a blanket from the overhead bin, reclined her seat, and closed her eyes. Ron smiled as he looked at her but he quickly got back to his laptop to try to catch up on his work.

Chapter Eight

Faukner's eyes began to close despite the work he was involved in on his laptop. Kraus was already asleep and he envied her ability to close her eyes and nod off. The air ride was smooth and the noise from the engines was a steady whirl. This was no commercial jet with seats so small you had to turn sideways to get into them. And there were no passengers behind him so he could recline almost to a horizontal position.

His mind wandered about his love of flying and the many trips he took as a young boy. His father was a career diplomat, and they were uprooted many times. He learned a lot about the world and he became fluent in five languages. He graduated in Scotland with a Ph.D. degree in political science. He held his own when his classmates were debating the role of the United States in world affairs.

He had relationships but they did not last. He enjoyed being the 'third wheel' as he observed the 'romance dance' his friends went through. The sudden death of his father created a whole different path for him, as the oldest, as he now had family responsibilities. But when life throws you a curve, just wait a minute and a correction will happen.

He was at the funeral home making arrangements for the burial. He lost his way in the building and wound up in a small room where two men were talking. The conversation was quite heated and he started to turn away when one of the men produced a gun. He was not sure why or whether the armed man was good or bad. He stepped into the room, grabbed the shooter's hand, and twisted the gun away. The second man punched the shooter who fell to the floor.

Four hours later he was on a plane surrounded by a small group of men and women flying to some foreign location. The police cleared him quickly after the man he saved showed them his identification. He was still not aware of the entire situation when a man, who later was identified as a CIA operative, talked him into going to a 'black site' or hidden location to hear more about careers in the CIA.

The 'black site' turned out to be a training center for new agents. He was interviewed by several people at different times. They came to the conclusion that the CIA was not for him. They instead introduced him to the NSA. Over the next ten years he rose to the rank of Assistant Director and, much like his father, he travelled all over the world. When General Campbell put in his urgent request for a seasoned operative who had computer skills and could communicate in several languages, he jumped at the chance.

Although he was single with no family of his own, he took easily to Marvin and surprisingly quickly to Maddy as well. His mind suddenly started putting codes together and he felt he had found the right one.

It was at this point that the flight steward gently woke him so he would put on his seat belt as they were about to land. Maddy was already up and belted in. She looked at him and smiled. "Thank you for letting me catch up on my sleep. I noticed you also took advantage of the flight. We will be on the ground in ten minutes or so. I feel like I owe you a breakfast."

Ron smiled. "Before I say yes, you're not a vegan or something weird like that?"

She laughed. "No, if I don't get my fill of bacon I am grumpy all day!"

The plane set down and Campbell called a quick meeting in the back of the plane. "Okay, we have found a location we believe fits the bill. There are two houses so we will split up. Each team will take a helicopter and investigate. Remember, we are racing a clock ticking toward the next disaster."

Ron spoke up. "Maddy and I will take one house."

"Good, then Marvin and I will take the other. Each team will have armed escorts, but try and maintain a calm presence. Good luck everyone."

The hunt for E1brad6L had brought them to the Florida Keys. Now they needed to find him before chapter four of the program destroyed another area.

Chapter Nine

General George Campbell and Marvin Robert Foster headed to the terminal building conference room to put together a plan for approaching the 'Bradley' house. Marvin filled in the General as to what to look for. They were joined by Major Bethany Younis, the General's personal aide. Bethany, called Beth, has been with the General for five years and they could read each other's body language.

"Marvin, this is Major Younis and she is my shadow. I can tell by the way she is standing there is trouble, big trouble, out there."

Beth saluted. "General, may I speak to you in private?"

Campbell shook his head. "Major, this is Marvin Foster. He is a remarkable young man. You can speak freely in front of him."

Beth was not sure what to do next. "Sir, this is classified information."

"It always is with us. Please, go ahead. I will take full responsibility."

Beth produced a file folder. "This is the latest action report. Russia has mobilized part of their army and all of their ships. There are reports that the entire Kremlin staff is heading to a safe bunker in Siberia. We have no idea why this is happening and you have been ordered back to Washington to deal with the situation."

Campbell sat silent for a minute. "Major, we are trying to stop the destruction of the earth. That is more important at this moment. You can travel with us and keep the channel open for further updates. If things turn really sour I will be able to break off and return to Washington."

The General continued with the planning. Marvin added new details. Bethany was just catching up with the situation. Two soldiers, heavily armed, joined the group as they prepared to leave for the 'Bradley' House.

Ron and Maddy were already in the air with their escorts, two heavily armed soldiers, and heading for the 'Palmer' House. The search teams had eliminated all the other persons of interest, so if neither of the houses panned out they would be back to square one. Maddy loved to fly but Ron kept complaining about the fact the helicopter had no wings so it could not really fly.

They read over the ground search report. "It says here that Palmer has two large towers in his backyard which could be used for directing sound waves and connecting to high power energy. With a background in computer science he invented a focus beam that can burn a hole in an armored tank at a great distance. Causing destruction like in Guam and O'Hare is a step up, and Palmer is talented enough to take that step."

Maddy looked over the details. "It says here Palmer was on the fast track until two years ago when his beam set off a chain reaction, causing an explosion, destroying the entire lab. Several people were hurt but none died. At the hearing, Palmer claimed that the accident was a blessing in disguise. Evan though he could cripple and destroy a military tank, his beam was too unstable. He retired from life."

Ron looked over the written report. "So you think someone stole his work and came up with a way to destroy large sections of the world. Was it for money or terrorism?"

"That's what we are going to find out. The pilot just signaled we are about to land. Better buckle up. I wouldn't want you to fall out."

Ron smiled. "Maddy, you really care about me."

"No. I just don't want to face all the paperwork I would have to fill out."

Just before they touched down the two soldiers jumped out and formed a defensive posture. Maddy and Rob got out and walked behind them. The area was a dead-end circle that backed up to EPA reserved land. There were five other houses on the street and many kids were approaching the foursome. Parents came running out of their houses to pull their children away. One of the parents had a rifle that looked like it was from World War II.

Maddy came out front. "Please, everyone, do not worry. We need to speak to one of your neighbors, Carl Palmer. He has not done anything wrong but we really need to see him."

The children continued to move back, with a little help from their parents. The armed soldiers lowered their weapons. Some of the children then ran to the helicopter hoping for free rides. Through all the confusion no one came forward to talk about Palmer.

Maddy stopped one of the parents. "Have you seen Mr. Palmer today? Do you know where he might be?"

The man lowered his rifle. "That Palmer is a strange duck. He keeps to himself and chases our kids off his property. His wife died about a year ago and they have no kids."

"Do you have any idea where he might be?"

"Most likely he's in the tunnel."

"What tunnel?"

The man looked around to see if anyone was listening. "You didn't hear this from me. He has an underground lab full of technical stuff and there have been a couple of explosions that shook some of our houses. I don't know what he does down there but you better get the bomb squad."

The man suddenly turned and hurried away. Maddy related the story to Ron. "I think we have found our E1brad6L."

Chapter Ten

Meanwhile General Campbell was concerned about Russian movements. He turned to the Major. "We have to take a side trip to Homestead Air Force Base where I can get a secure line."

"I'll tell the flight crew."

"I have to speak with my source and find out what has 'poked the black bear'."

As they headed to the helicopter, Marvin questioned the Major. "What does 'poke the black bear' mean?"

Beth Younis smiled. "That is old folks speak much like you have young folks speak on your texting. Russia was called the big black bear during the Cold War. The idea was to allow Russia to be quiet like a hibernating bear and not to disturb or poke it."

Marvin still had a puzzled look. "Why don't you just say leave Russia alone?"

"Why do you say OMG or LOL or other letters?"

They boarded the helicopter and headed off. When they landed they were met by a squad of soldiers and a staff car. There were salutes all around as the General and his party made their way to the communications center.

"Major, get me Lars."

Marvin turned to Beth but she answered before he could ask. "Lars is a friend of the Generals, in a sort of off-the-record wau."

Lars came on the line. "General George, I haven't talked with you in quite a while. I had a feeling I would be getting this call."

"Lars Arvidson, my favorite Scandinavian trader. How goes the Russia trade?"

Lars wanted to get right to it. "General George, you did not contact me on this line to find out how many LEGO blocks I shipped to Moscow."

"I need to know why Russia is mobilizing. Who or what has caused the panic?"

Ivol laughed. "Why it's you. They are responding to your moves."

The General was caught by surprise. "What the hell did we do?"

"Some of the hard-liner Russians think that the so-called game that is destroying areas and people is a cover for a new weapon you have. They fear that Moscow is next to be destroyed. They are evacuating certain structures in the capital."

"Lars, believe me, that is not the case. We are trying to stop this game before there is any other damage. We have lost Guam, O'Hare and Japan's Kure."

"It could be a that is a sacrifice you are making so it looks like you are telling the truth."

Campbell lowered his head into his hands for a minute. Beth moved Marvin to the other side of the room. "Lars, what do you suggest?"

The speaker went quiet for a moment. "There is a highly decorated hero of the people visiting Cuba and giving speeches. Perhaps you could add him to your group, be totally transparent, and let him communicate with the Kremlin."

George leaned back and looked at Beth across the room. He knew it was the only way to handle the situation. "Okay, send me the information on this guy and we will ask him to join us."

"I have already done so. I hope your family is well."

"Wife and kids are great. And your family?"

"I just got married again. I hope three is a lucky number."

They both laughed. "Goodbye, old friend."

Ron and Maddy were still trying to find someone to help them find the missing Palmer. The neighbors had closed and locked their doors. The dead-end street was silent and had the appearance of one of those horror movies with all the shades pulled down, and not even a squirrel or bird could be heard or seen. Maddy decided to knock on the door of the closest house.

"Hello! We are not here to hurt anyone. We are looking for help in finding Carl Palmer. Please do not be afraid."

The door opened just enough so Maddy could see a woman. "Go away!"

"We are not here to hurt anyone. Why are you so afraid?"

The women opened the door further, stuck her head out, and looked to the right and then to the left. "You are not ICE?"

Now it made sense. There were house cleaners and repairmen in some of the houses and they probably did not have proper papers. "Please. We are not from ICE. I promise we will not report anything we see."

The door opened a little wider and a man, holding the World War II rifle, was now visible. "How can we trust you?"

Ron took out his cell. "Yes, let me speak to the Director."

After a brief conversation he handed the cell to the man. "He has offered total immunity and asked that I join your team. It is a good offer."

Ron, Maddy, and now Diego Perez were on the hunt for Palmer.

Chapter Eleven

The summons to the meeting was only one paragraph but every minister dropped what they were doing and headed out. They met in the private office of President Vladimir Putin. Some worried they might be under review and were being replaced. Others thought there must be yet another challenge to Mother Russia. They waited in silence knowing whatever they said would be recorded.

Few Americans are aware that the Kremlin is actually a small city surrounded by thick walls. Built around 1485, there are many other buildings that are open for tourists to visit. The Kremlin Palace, now used as the residence of the Russian President, is thought of as the seat of government much like the American White House is. Views from the Palace include the Moskva River, Saint Basil's Cathedral, Red Square, and the Alexander Gardens. The lower-case kremlin refers to the small area inside the walls and the capitalized Kremlin refers to the Palace and seat of government. Most people use the capitalized Kremlin for both.

Five Americans are buried inside the Kremlin for their roles assisting the growth of Communism since the great Russian Civil War after World War I. John Reed played a major role in the success of the Bolsheviks and C. E. Ruthenberg founded the Communist party in America. The area just behind the wall also has the remains of Joseph Stalin after he was removed from Lenin's tomb.

Like European highly decorated and ornate government buildings, the Kremlin was built as an attempt to surpass the French palace at Versailles. With gold encrusted statues and walls lined with gold stripes, there was nothing in the building that would resemble what a true Communist building should look like.

"Gentlemen, Vladimir Vladimirovich Putin!"

Since World War II all power was centralized in Russia which was now called the Russian Federation. Everyone stood as Putin entered and took his place at the head of a long, narrow table. In the area from his seat down to the middle of the table, no one was allowed to sit. All the ministers and officials were crowded into the other end of the twenty-foot table. Guards were present to protect the President and to remove anyone Putin dismissed.

"My President, this note is upsetting and very short on information. What is this great crisis we face?"

Putin opened a file and began to address the emergency. "You have all been made aware of this American game that is destroying areas around the world. We have verified that the Guam village, the airport O'Hare, and the Kure port in Japan have all been destroyed by some very powerful and unknown weapon. The Americans claim it is an out-of-control AI product."

The group all nodded. The Deputy Prime Minister agreed. "Yes, my President."

Putin stood, extended his arms, and learned forward using his hands and arms as supports. "I have reason to believe that this is all a clever cover for an imminent attack on Russia under the guise of runaway science."

The entire room began to come alive with accusations being thrown around. Some wanted to launch a pre-emptive strike while others pushed a more cautioned approach. But Putin had already taken action. "I have raised the threat level to three. I have ordered the Intelligence Service to call upon all our people secretly living in the United States to find out what is going on. All submarines are in planned zones."

Heads turned and now the debate started about when to take a stronger course of action. Just then a guard handed Putin a note. He read it and immediately turned and left the room. In a private office, Putin met with Lars Arvidson who had just hung up with General Campbell.

"Mr. President, I have taken the steps you outlined. Based on my conversation, I believe the rogue AI project is not a camouflage of an American first strike."

Putin shook his head. "Thank you Comrade Arvidson. I want to know immediately anything you find out, no matter how small."

"Yes, Mr. President."

"And Lars, you had better be right."

Chapter Twelve

"VLADIVOSTOK!!"

Marvin, sitting in the rear of the helicopter, let out a scream. "I figured it out! Vladivostok is the next target!"

Ivan Boris Kuznetsov, recently added to the group from a speaking engagement in Cuba, turned to Marvin. "Does this mean Russia is the target?"

The General clicked on his microphone and called the Command Center. "Tell them it's Vladivostok. I don't know what we can do about it but at least they can start evacuating the city."

Ivan shook his head. "So this is the boy genius who developed this killing machine of a program."

Beth turned on her microphone. "No Admiral Kuznetsov, he is the boy genius who is trying to stop the killing machine. We are still searching for the designer."

Ivan had arrived by special flight from Cuba to Homestead Base and before he could say hello and meet the team, he was pulled onto a helicopter that was heading to the Keys. Campbell did his best to update the Admiral but the copter was too loud. The only thing that was clear was Ivan's desire to stop the program.

Admiral Kuznetsov was a hero of Mother Russia. He led the navy on many practices and worked well with China and North Korea as he spoke both languages. On the last maneuver, a North Korean destroyer accidentally rammed a Russian submarine which quickly sank taking with it one hundred and thirty-two crew and observers. But the disaster was not a tragedy thanks to the Admiral.

Knowing the dangers of joint exercises, Kuznetsov ordered two rescue submersibles to be on station. Normally such rescue ships would be in port and need at least two days to get to the scene. Now the ships were two hours away and could begin operations immediately. The Admiral had lines attached to the damaged sub along with ballast membranes to keep it afloat as long as possible. All crew and observers were saved and sensitive information was removed. Finally the damaged sub was towed back to port. Kuznetsov was proclaimed a Hero of Russia.

Ivan, Campbell, Beth, and Marvin set down in a parking lot across from the Bradley home. MP's from Homestead had already cordoned off the area and a large crowd had already formed along the metal barriers. They left the copter at a run and met up at the front door of the house. It was quite a scene for the media. Ivan in his Russian uniform, George in his American uniform, Beth in uniform, and a sixteen-year-old kid in jeans.

The door opened before they could knock. George took the lead. "We need to speak with Mr. Bradley, it is of national importance!"

From behind the door stepped a young girl, about sixteen, with blond hair and blue eyes wearing jeans with more holes than Swiss cheese and a top with a picture of Taylor Swift. "What do you want?"

"I am General Campbell and we are on an urgent mission. We need to speak with your father."

"My father is Thomas Lewis. He is at work."

"Where does he work?"

"At the auto dealership where he is a mechanic."

Ivan pressed forward. "Please, this is taking too long. Does your father have special computer skills? Does he program games and such?"

The girl looked confused. "My dad has trouble using his cell phone. I think we are the only house that still uses a landline."

Marvin pushed his way forward. One look and he was totally captivated. "Ah…I mean…hello, I am Marvin. Where is Mr. Bradley?"

The girl smiled and brushed her hair back with her hand. "He is in New York."

Marvin was having trouble keeping calm. "When…when…will he be back?"

"Henry Bradley died one hundred and seventy years ago. He is our family founder and he built this house which is why it's called the Bradley House. No one named Bradley lives here."

"But you are a Bradley?"

"Yes, and proud of it. Every person in this family has Bradley for a middle name, even the women."

The General then started to walk away. "Well, this is a dead end. Hopefully Maddy and Ron are having more luck finding Palmer. Right now we have to get Marvin back to the base so he can work out the timing and position of the attack on Vladivostok."

As they started to walk away the girl yelled out. "Nice to meet you. My name is Emily, Emily Bradley Lewis."

Marvin turned. "Hi, I'm Marvin Foster. Are you online? Are you into games?"

"I love them. Search for WICKED742."

"Thanks. When I get some free time I'll try to connect."

Although the adults went away unhappy and worried, Marvin was bright and thrilled. He knew he still had to pinpoint the attack on Vladivostok, but even that now felt different. Beth noticed the change in Marvin and smiled. Ivan and George were discussing ways to evacuate that part of Vladivostok that might be hit. Panic would be just as damaging as the attack.

As he prepared to return to base, a call came through from Ron. "General, we ran into a little problem but it's cleared up. We are working with a Mexican worker named Diego Perez. We need to get him a green card ASAP. What happened down there?"

"We struck out. Bradley has been dead for over a hundred and fifty years or so. We hope Marvin will have the coordinates soon. Keep me informed."

"Will do."

It was now up to Marvin to pinpoint the location in Vladivostok. Unfortunately, his mind was not totally immersed in the task.

Chapter Thirteen

Maddy and Ron sat down with Diego to get background on Carl Palmer. The house was small but comfortable. The kitchen was decorated with items from Mexico and there was a large pot cooking on the stove. The aroma caused all of them to wish for a bowlful right there and then. Off to the left was a living room with a television larger than all the monitors at Command Central. As they sat down on the sofa they could hear music, or what they call music today.

Ron took out a notepad. "Diego, thank you for helping us. What can you tell me about Palmer?"

"My wife cleans houses and you would be surprised at the things people say, not realizing there is another person in the room."

Maddy nodded. "Women. We are the invisible caretakers of the world."

Diego laughed. "Women. A necessity with a large price."

Ron smiled. "Okay. Let's get back to Palmer."

"Carl Palmer bought the house about fifteen years ago. The house was built in the 1960s just when Cuba and Russia were putting missiles in play. The original owner had a fallout shelter put in without getting a permit. Not even the Florida government knows about it. But they still panicked over the crisis and moved away."

"Do you know what Palmer does for a living? We did a deep dive but only came up with a computer business."

Diego smiled. "You would find out more by going into the neighborhood for information. Not everything can be found with a computer."

"Okay. What are we missing?"

"Palmer's company was called 'SkyDreams'."

That bit of information caused Maddy and Ron to suddenly sit up straight and push for more. "He ran 'SkyDreams'. Did he do any software development?"

"He invented computer games and software that links cell towers. His last invention is a 'tower' that only sits three inches above ground but can send and receive signals around the world using satellites. He had a department that did nothing but AI. His company was named 'Bright Reliable AI Development'."

Ron leaned back and started to scribble on the notepad. "The initials would be B. R. A. D. just like in E1brad6L. Have you ever seen inside the fallout shelter?"

"Just once when he first moved in. There are all kinds of technological equipment and banks of computers."

Ron looked at Maddy. "I think we have found our E1brad6L. We need to get into that fallout shelter ASAP."

He picked up his cell and called Campbell. "General, we hit paydirt. All the pieces fell into place. Palmer is probably hiding out in a fallout shelter. We need to get in. What do you suggest?"

An hour later a contingent of military, along with the FBI, ATF, State and Local police had surrounded the hatch leading to the shelter. Welders cut through the door and armed men descended. They arrived outside a door leading into the central chamber. They pounded on the door. "Open up!! We have a court order to enter the premises!! We will breach the door if you refuse."

There was no answer. The soldiers planted explosives and quickly left the area. There was a loud explosion and smoke and shrapnel came flying out the hatch like cannon fodder. Wearing protective masks, the soldiers went back down and found the door had been vaporized. They proceeded, slowly, weapons ready, into the chamber.

The men radioed back. "All clear. Send the inspection team."

Ron and Maddy joined the others and began inspecting the chamber. Off to the left was a storeroom loaded with dry food and meals ready-to-eat. There were jugs of water and an entire wall of first aid materials. To the right was a bedroom with four beds and pictures of outside scenes. The center of the chamber housed the technical computer materials Diego had talked about.

But there was no Palmer. Ron and Maddy were positive they had found where E1brad6L developed the program but without Palmer they still were unable to stop the game. Once back up top, they were met by Diego. "I had a thought. Palmer talked about a mini spa which contained a sauna, hot tub, and small workout area. I jotted down the location."

Maddy got the car and the two drove carefully to the location Diego gave them. It was a small strip mall with five stores. The one in the middle was named 'Spritz-Away'. They figured that would be the place to start. The door was locked but there were lights on inside. They knocked but no answer. They pounded on the door and finally got a response.

"Go away!! We're closed except to private customers!! This is private property!! Who are you and what do you want?"

"We are looking for Carl Palmer. Have you seen him?"

"What do you want with him?"

Maddy tried to look inside. "We need to talk with him about 'World Obliteration'."

"I knew someone would be coming. Now I can get the revenge I want."

Ron stated the obvious. "So you are Carl Palmer."

Maddy came right out with it. "You are destroying property and people for some kind of revenge?"

"No. I want to find the person who developed that game so I can kill him, and you are going to help me."

Ron shook his head. "But you developed the game."

"No. That program killed my son and daughter-in-law and I want him dead. Now get inside and tell me everything you know."

Once inside Maddy and Ron were faced with Palmer waving a shotgun, and by the look on his face he was ready to use it. "Now tell me everything you found out. That bastard killed my son and daughter-in-law. They were at O'Hare Airport. They never found their bodies."

Ron stepped in front of Maddy acting like a shield. "We have teams searching for the developer and we have some people trying to shut the program down. We are sorry about your loss but we don't have any information you could use to find the man. All we know is the handle he uses which is E1brad6L. Does that mean anything to you?"

Palmer lowered the gun. "Yes, when I was CEO of 'SkyDreams' I was contacted by someone using that handle. At first he proposed kids' games. Then he came by with a wild game proposal that was filled with death and destruction. I turned him down and that is the last I heard from him."

Maddy felt better with the gun lowered. "Did he use any description of his whereabouts? Like a beach he could see from his house."

Palmer put the gun down. "Now that you mention it, we talked about the Keys and how we were neighbors. I have some correspondence back at my house from when he developed those kid games."

Ron cleared his throat. "Before we head back, there is something we need to tell you about that bomb shelter you own."

Chapter Fourteen

The three were headed back to Palmer's fallout shelter. Palmer was not happy to hear about what happened to his shelter. "The government better pay for the damage!"

Maddy tried to change the subject. "What kind of correspondence do you have and where do you keep it?"

Ron called the General and told him all was clear. He filled Campbell in and asked that the soldiers be withdrawn from the shelter. When they arrived at Palmer's house they found that the military had tried their best to clean up the before they withdrew. The three went down the hatch and sat in the kitchen area. Maddy cleaned off the table from the dust of the explosion and found an electric kettle. "I'll make some coffee. Where do you keep it?"

"In the cabinet labeled breakfast."

Maddy opened the cabinet and discovered four shelves filled with coffee cans. It looked like

Palmer was prepared for a stay of decades, not just days or weeks. "Any pastry?"

"Just the 'add water and bake' kind. They are nutritious but taste awful."

As the coffee brewed they sat at the kitchen table. "We need to know the background of this E1brad6L person and how much of the game he told you about."

Palmer explained the backstory to the game development. As the owner of SkyDreams he published a lot of both entertainment and commercial programs. E1brad6L had contacted him about a game he developed for kids. It had a bunch of cute animals and the places they lived and you had to match the animal to its habitat. All the contact was over the internet, so the two never met. There were so many kid,s games on the market that there would not be much profit in producing another.

It was then that the idea for 'World Obliteration' was first brought up to Palmer. To make money you had to appeal to the pre- and grown teen. That would mean something with a lot of explosions, shootings, and gore. E1brad6L seemed anxious to try out some program ideas and submitted the destruction of an army base. The programming exchanges became increasingly bloody.

Maddy brought over the coffee. "So you never met him. Did you ever get a look at his face over the net? Did you ever trace his IP address?"

Palmer sipped his drink. "No. I'm pretty good online but even I couldn't trace the origins of the maniac."

"Did you ever speak with him?"

"Once. I was worried kids would change the code and make the game even more bloody, but he said he installed a double key into the program with a failsafe. If you don't press the right key, the program will not shut down. Therefore no one can tamper with the code."

Ron's cell rang. "Hello. This is Ron."

"This is George. We're about to leave the Keys. Are you ready to go back to Command Central? Marvin is still working on a Vladivostok location for the next attack and he needs some programs to try to locate it."

Ron continued. "Palmer's correspondence was little help but he did confirm the use of a double key security system. I hate to say it but I think we are back to square one."

"And yet you said it. We will be ready to leave in an hour."

Ron hung up and turned to Palmer. "Thank you for your help. Is there anything we can do for you besides send people to fix your fallout shelter?"

"No. Forget it. The shelter is not much good given the power of today's weapons."

Marvin came running into the temporary field headquarters. "I've got it!"

"You know where the attack will be?"

"Yes. And I think I found E1brad6L!"

Chapter Fifteen

Everyone within earshot came running to the field command center. Ron and Maddy just made it in time. Ivan was present since the attack was targeting Vladivostok. Most of the world was convinced the program was AI-made and not the fault of the U.S. military. They still had to convince Ivan. Marvin put the calculations on a large whiteboard. There were so many people crowded around the board, there was barely room for air.

General Campbell patted Marvin on the back and Beth kissed him on the cheek. Marvin was taking in all the congratulations and began to strut around. "Yes, it all adds up. We have at least two days before the attack, so evacuations are possible."

Maddy was at the table looking at the calculations. "Everyone, stop what you're doing. There is a problem here."

The crowd, much like a wave, moved over to Maddy's location. "Marvin, you are one of the brightest computer people I have ever worked with.

Unfortunately, your simple math brings tears to my eyes. How did you come up with the coordinates?"

Marvin was feeling a little panicky. "I took the program's symbols and values and put them into the formula I used…"

"Did the computer do the calculations?"

Marvin could feel the panic growing. "No. I was out in the field, sitting in the back seat of a car, doing the math in my head."

"In this case you subtracted six from ten and got four."

"Yes…"

"But you needed to borrow from the ten for the column on the right. That left the actual number a nine. And six from nine is…"

"Three."

Ron began to run the math. "Here is a division error. Let's enter the whole formula into the computer."

Everyone watched as numbers flashed on the screen. The values were far different than Marvin's total. "Let's plot the coordinates again."

Maddy looked at the crowd. "Marvin's original formula came out with coordinates of 40.3399 degrees North and 127.5161 degrees East.

That puts the zone in Vladivostok. The new numbers are 43.1332 degrees North and 131.9113 degrees East."

Campbell quickly brought up a map on the monitor. "It's not Vladivostok. It's **North Korea**!!"

The only one happy about that was Ivan. He immediately sent a coded message to the Kremlin. Campbell called Lars and gave him the news. The crisis with Russia was over but a new one had risen with North Korea. Campbell went into a private area for security reasons and took out a satellite phone.

"This is General Campbell. I need to speak with the President. NOW!"

After a short wait, the President came on the line. "General Campbell, I understand we now have the location of the attack and the location of the creator of the game. I'll contact Putin and we will work out some…"

"Sorry to interrupt sir, but that will not be necessary. There was a correction in the target. It is not Vladivostok. It is North Korea."

The phone line went silent. Campbell could hear the President's breathing which was very erratic. *"General, are you sure? This will be a disaster of world proportions. Get your team on the fastest plane and meet me in the White House!"*

Campbell came out of the area. "Major Younis, get us the fastest plane available. I don't care if you have to throw people off. Everyone head for the gate. We are leaving now."

Ivan seemed to speak for everyone. "What is the problem? I do not have to go as Russia is not in any danger."

Campbell walked up to Ivan and stood two feet away. "Everyone is going either on their own or with help from these soldiers."

And so the group headed for the tarmac. And what a group it was:

*General George Campbell, aide to the President and liaison from the Pentagon.

*Major Bethany Younis, personal aide to General Campbell.

*Ronald Faulkner, Assistant Director NSA, and Homeland Security liaison.

*Madeline Kraus, Assistant Director Cyber Security.

*Ivan Boris Kuznetsov, Aide to Vladimir Puttin and liaison with the Kremlin.

*Marvin Robert Foster, age sixteen.

The plane was up in the air and heading to Washington, D. C., and a meeting with the President. Meanwhile in the White House the President was calling members of his cabinet and other military personnel to join him in the meeting. It was all-hands-on-deck as people were pulled out of meetings or other work. Finally military police collected the Speaker of the House and the President Pro Tempore of the Senate.

It felt like the longest plane ride, and despite the people on board you could hear a fly land. While most looked at charts, maps, and statistics, Marvin continued to concentrate on his choice for E1brad6L. He went over his figures for the new coordinates and when the next attack would take place. They had two, maybe three days, to evacuate or come up with the second key. And he wondered what there was about North Korea that caused such panic.

The only saving grace was that the media had not noticed what was happening. But that media blackout would only last so long.

Chapter Sixteen

Activity at the White House was frenetic and tense. The Situation Room is where all national security threats are hashed out. There is strict protocol with both the President and Vice-President in attendance. Communications are at the highest level and with the push of a button the President could be in touch with any world leader. Sometimes Presidents feel as if the Situation Room is more important than the Oval Office.

President Warner Phillips was in his second term with just two years left. He had weathered a number of storms including a deep divide between political parties. Several of his staff were testing the waters for the next election although the smart money was on his Vice-President, Susan Mason. Her performance pushing back on Putin and Xi earned her a strong reputation. She also settled a nationwide teachers' strike.

Another candidate on staff was William Farmer, Director of the C. I. A. Before taking on the chief spy post he was a highly successful Governor and Senator from New York. Vegas oddsmakers were betting on a Mason/Farmer ticket. President Phillips was silent on all things political and had hoped his last two years would be as a caretaker. The news about the North Korean target shook all that up.

Everyone had their place. Marvin was included due to his knowledge of the program and his algorithm that predicted what the next target would be. He was aware of the Situation Room from the news but was not sure how things operated. Sadly, his public-school education never covered this level of government. Beth sat next to him and answered his questions.

The President entered and everyone stood. The tension was so thick that blood pressure was in four digits. "Ladies and gentlemen, we have a very difficult decision to make. I will turn the meeting over to General Campbell. General."

Campbell had items posted on the five monitors in the room. "According to Marvin Foster, the next attack will be in North Korea. The specific coordinates place the hit at Punggye-ri. It will destroy everything within a radius of two hundred and fifty miles. We have time to warn the North Koreans but…"

The President took over. "Punggye-ri is the center of North Korea's nuclear and ballistic program. This attack will wipe out their ability to develop future weapons and all but end their ability to reach far away targets. Since the world leaders know about this program, we hope they would understand our position and the United States would not be blamed. But North Korea does not deal in reality. They will still want revenge against us."

Ron brought up an idea. "We could tell the North Koreans and they could evacuate in time, but that might not be the best thing to do for us."

Marvin was upset hearing his friend Ron talk about not evacuating the site. He leaned over to Beth. "I don't understand why we do not want to evacuate all those people."

Beth whispered in his ear. "Who creates those missiles and bombs?"

"Scientists and military guys."

Beth paused. "If we destroy every weapon they have, what will they do?"

"Make new ones."

"And that's why we might not want to allow them to evacuate their personnel."

Marvin was just beginning to take it all in. When he first arrived he had believed they should just tell North Korea and evacuate all the people. Now he was beginning to see that the decision was far more complicated. "Beth, how do you decide what to do?"

"You sometimes wind up hating yourself."

The C.I.A. Director spoke next. "We have to consider that the North Koreans are fanatics and will do things that civilized world countries would never do. Even with the area destroyed, North Korea has the third largest army in the world. Given the fact they had been pushed back into the stone age, weapons-wise, they would most likely invade South Korea to gain back their standing."

Vice-President Mason had another approach. "Marvin's original plot put the attack at Vladivostok. We can release those coordinates and make it seem as if Russia is the target. Therefore it will be his bad math that caused us to miss the real target of North Korea."

Phillips nodded. "That is one way to go. But will Russia go along with the subterfuge?"

Ivan spoke up. "Russia will do what it has to in order to make the world safer."

Joint Chief of Staff Manning started to laugh. "I don't suppose Russia's motive to go along would be a weakened North Korea would need to rely even more on them."

Ivan shook his head. "We will do what is best for the world."

Conversations between individuals began to erupt more often and they got louder and louder. It was chaos. Marvin did not know who to listen to and who to believe. The President called for quiet. Campbell gave a list to the officer at the computer who typed in the information which was then brought up on the monitors.

"As I see it, these are our choices: First, we let the attack happen destroying all weapons and humans within a two-hundred-mile radius. The brain trust who builds these weapons would perish. We release the false coordinates and supply food and medicine as we would do for any disaster. The second choice is to get the people out and let the weapons be destroyed. And the third choice is we help the Koreans evacuate and save as much of their technology as they can."

The side conversation picked up again. Suddenly a phone rang and everyone stopped talking. "This is the President. What? Are you sure? Send all the research you have."

Campbell asked what everyone wanted to ask. "What has happened?"

The President was shaking. "The President of South Korea, who has been following our deliberations, told me once the weapons are destroyed he will invade North Korea and reunite the peninsula under South Korean rule."

"Damn! That will start a third world war!"

Different views and ideas were expressed. Marvin was totally lost and hoped he could get out of the room and find a quiet place. Beth reached over. "Marvin, I think that is our cue to leave."

Chapter Seventeen

The entire group left the Situation Room and most headed for the cafeteria. The President went to the Oval office and Ivan Boris Kuznetsov headed for the Russian Embassy. Once there he marched into the Russian Ambassador's Office despite efforts to stop him. The Ambassador was in a meeting with three other people. "Who are you? What are you doing in my office? Guards!!"

"I am Ivan Kuznetsov. Do you know what it means when I say 'Krasnaya Zvezda"?"

The Ambassador stopped and had a panicked look. "Of course, Comrade. I know what that means. Alex, take Comrade Ivan to the secure communications room, immediately!!"

The new Russian Federation had stopped using the title 'Comrade' and it only existed in situations of critical importance. The person using the phrase 'Krasnaya Zvezda', or 'Red Star', was standing in for President Putin and could not be questioned or denied. When Ivan entered the communications area the person in charge ordered everyone out and sealed the room. Ivan sat at a special computer and entered a password.

"This is Comrade Ivan Boris Kuznetsov. Pass me to the President's Office."

"We are notifying President Putin of your call. Please give us a few minutes."

Putin came on the air. "Ivan, this is Vladimir, what do you have to report?"

"The Americans are leaning towards allowing the attack on North Korea. Punggye-ri will be obliterated along with their top scientists. They will claim Vladivostok was the target and some kid messed up the math. If you prepare emergency aid and ship it to the border, we can then be on scene and can become their major partner."

Putin rubbed his hands together. "With the Ukraine war going slowly we need a big win. Get back to the meeting and tell them I agree with their plan."

"One other thing Comrade Vladimir. We are about to capture the person who developed the program. He will be a most useful addition to our cyber team. We should activate some of our in-place people who are undercover in the United States so they can make the grab."

"You have my approval. Get moving."

Marvin was trying to enjoy lunch but seemed to have no appetite. Maddy walked over carrying her tray. "Marvin, may I join you? The food here is really excellent."

"Please, sit down. My brain has been twisted around. I cannot believe some of the things that were discussed."

Maddy touched his shoulder. "Marvin, you have been thrust into the real world like jumping into a pool in the deep end. And you don't know how to swim.'

"Yes, that's exactly how I feel. I need to figure things out."

Beth approached carrying her tray. "Hi, mind if I join you? The food here is really excellent."

Maddy and Marvin started to laugh. "We just said the same thing."

Beth touched his shoulder. "Marvin, the best thing you can do now is to talk about it. There will be no judgment here. We just want to alleviate your fears and support your feelings."

Marvin nodded. "I can understand destroying all their weapons and equipment but I can't understand how we can stand by and have hundreds, thousands, of people perish. They have done nothing to us. They have families and friends."

Beth looked at Maddy and then Marvin. "In the movies the hero saves innocent people. But in real life that is not always possible. I am sure you have heard the term 'big picture'. It is the tough reality we sometimes have to face."

Maddy picked up the conversation. "There is a story people tell about an incident that happened during World War II in England. To this day we do not know if it really happened, but there is enough proof to make it real."

"What happened?"

"The British were being bombed day and night until they broke the NAZI war code. The first thing they heard was about a major attack on one of the cities designed to kill every man, woman, and child in the town. If they evacuated the people the NAZIs would know their code had been broken and England would lose a valuable tool to beat Hitler. Central Command debated it over and over. The final decision was to let the raid happen, killing their own countrymen."

"Were a lot of people killed?"

"Yes, hundreds, and the town was destroyed. But that is where the 'big picture' comes in. With the code broken, the NAZIs were finally stopped and some of the other targets were saved. Thousands and thousands of lives were spared. Was it the right decision? That will be debated forever."

Marvin looked at Beth. "Would you have made the same decision?"

"In hindsight and being able to put together facts they couldn't have known, I would have made a different decision. But if I were there, at the time, I might have agreed."

Marvin picked up his fork. "So it's all a matter of the situation at the time. I know North Korea keeps threatening the world and this attack is the price we pay for making the world safer."

"Are you feeling any better?"

Marvin dropped the fork. "Absolutely not. But I can live with it. Now we have to find E1brad6L before anyone else has to die."

Chapter Eighteen

Ronald Faulkner was glued to the monitor as he pinpointed North Korean facilities in the expected target area. It was one thing to destroy weapons systems and materials of war, but it was something very different to hit private homes, schools, and hospitals. He was also trying to determine what the casualty numbers would be. He did not notice Maddy walking in.

"Ron, what is the bottom line?"

Ron looked up and a feeling of warmth filled his body. "Hi Maddy, how did it go with Marvin?"

Maddy shook her head. "We talked him off the ledge but I'm afraid it will stay with him for a very long time. When does the conference continue?"

"In about thirty minutes. I did the calculations and it isn't pretty. Are we prepared to take so many innocent lives?"

"War is horrible."

Ron leaned back. "But we are not at war."

With just fifteen minutes before the conference was to begin, the rest of the members began to arrive. They all headed into the Situation Room and waited for the President. Marvin was there with a folder that read 'Russian Negotiations and Treaties'.

Ivan Kuznetsov walked in. "I have spoken with my President and he is willing to support whatever press release you authorize."

The President was next to enter. "I think we are all up to date on the choices. Unless there is something new to add, I think we can vote on action."

Ivan raised his hand. "Mr. President, I have talked with President Putin and he has agreed to support whatever this group decides. He will announce that the target is Vladivostok and he will begin an evacuation to make it look real."

"That is good news, Mr. Kuznetsov. So I guess that settles the matter."

Just then Marvin raised his hand. The others in the room looked puzzled and the President had hoped to finish this business. "Marvin, I know you are new to all this but when the discussions are complete we take a vote. So unless what you have to say is critical…"

Marvin stood up. "Mr. President, as you say I am new to all this but I am also a diligent researcher. I have read this file Mr. Faulkner gave me and it has raised a troubling thought."

General Campbell spoke up. "Mr. President, please excuse my computer wizard. Being young he has not had the experience…"

Marvin pushed forward. "I'm sorry, General Campbell, but I have been told that due diligence is the bedrock of decisions."

There was uneasiness in the room. Beth finally broke the silence. "Mr. President, what could it hurt to hear him out?"

The President nodded. "Okay, Marvin, what is this important input you have?"

The pressure and the spotlight were directly on Marvin. "Ladies and gentlemen, I am new to this and I have not attended many conferences. I believe that until the last person is heard the group should hold off on any decisions."

General Campbell let out a loud sigh. "You are right. Please continue."

Marvin pulled up a computer chart. "On the left you will see how many conferences and treaties the Russians have discussed and agreed to. On the right you see how many of those agreements were broken by Russia. In the center is something I have taken from Herbert Leyland, former Ambassador to Russia and adviser to the last three Presidents."

Campbell nodded. "Yes, I worked with Leyland. He was right on about Russian motives and movements."

Marvin continued. "Leyland said that if you read Russian history, looking closely at Russian treaties and agreements, you would find the Russians break their agreements eighty five percent of the time. So if we discount their promise to support us, we are left with a double cross. The Russians would only agree because they could show proof that we knew North Korea was the target and we were prepared to let thousands of people die. It would be a double win for Russia."

There was so much tension in the room you could not walk through it. Heads started nodding up and down and individuals began passing notes. Ivan did not know what to do. He tried to save the situation by promising that Putin wanted to show good faith so sanctions on his country would be lifted. It looked as if they were back to square one.

The President called for silence. "This young man has the wisdom of someone who has had years of experience in diplomacy."

Ron called for a tabling of the discussion. "I worked with Marvin on the timing of the attack. It will not be until three days from now. I suggest we use the first day to find E1brad6L and try and stop the program. That will leave us two days to warn the North Koreans and evacuate."

The President gave the final words. "Get it done!"

Marvin's heart was beating faster than the speed of a race car in NASCAR. Perspiration saturated his clothes and ran down his forehead. He could not catch his breath so he could not speak. Maddy and Beth took him over to the White House infirmary, which is really a miniature hospital, and the nurse gave him a shot to calm him down.

Beth sat beside him as he lay on a bed. "You did it. Everyone is talking about the genius who kept the United States from making a major mistake. Now we have to find E1brad6L and see if we can stop this program."

Marvin could rest his body but not his mind.

Chapter Nineteen

Although the White House dining area was much more than a cafeteria, Ron sat alone there facing a new deadline of twenty-four hours. They had tried for weeks to find E1brad6L and were unsuccessful. He was so engrossed in thought he did not notice when Maddy came along.

"Marvin is resting. I'll wake him in an hour and we can begin the search. What's that you're eating?"

Ron looked up. For the first time he noticed her smile and her eyes. She was always a bright part of his day and he began to think of her in a different way. But they were new friends and there was no time to do anything except find the creator of that game.

"It's pasta, ziti, with butter and breadcrumbs. It is quite good; you should try it."

"Sorry but pasta is not on my menu card."

Ron smiled. "If anything, you need not worry about eating pasta. You look…"

"I look what?"

"Okay, I think I am about to dig myself into a rather large hole."

Maddy laughed. "I promise I will not sue you for sexual harassment. Finish your thought."

Ron shook his head. "I was about to say you look like a fashion model. When you walk you look so sophisticated as if you are part of the wealthy one percent."

"I'm not sure that's a compliment. You men have it so easy because we women forgive your big stomachs and aging faces. We have to be perfect."

Now Ron was ready for a fight. "Hold on. We guys are just as worried about our looks as you girls are. I'll have to hit the gym for an extra day just to work off this pasta."

Maddy laughed. "From where I sit you have nothing to go to the gym for."

Ron had a surprised look on his face. "Are you flirting with me?"

She was equally surprised. "Weren't you flirting with me?

The two sat in silence. Beth came by with two salads, sat down, and gave one salad to Maddy. "I had them put the dressing on the side."

Much to Beth's confusion Ron and Maddy broke into laughter. Beth looked around and did not see anything that would be funny. "Are you two okay?"

Ron went back to his pasta and Maddy started to eat her salad. They both had wide smiles on their faces.

Marvin was finally awake and headed to the computer area to finish working on his unveiling of E1brad6L. He was joined by Ron, Maddy, and the General.

"Okay, Marvin, let us see what you have for us."

Marvin pulled up some kind of code chart. "First I used a cypher code to rearrange the words, and one version put the EL at the end of 'brad' giving us Bradley. Next I used the numbers as an age and gave me 16."

"Are you saying that the sixteen-year-old girl we met two days ago is the person we are looking for?"

Marvin continued. "When the General and I interviewed this Emily she gave us the story of her father being an auto repair person who does not have the skills to develop the game. She never mentioned her mother."

The General asked Ron about his follow up interview with Emily Lewis. "When Maddy and I interviewed the Lewis girl she gave us an entirely different story about her father. She changed his occupation and even changed her father's name from Thomas to Gene. I had my assistant dig deeper into the Lewis family."

"What did he find?"

"Gene Lewis, the father, had a nervous breakdown and is living off the grid in a berm hut. Rosa Lewis, the mother, is a nurse in a Senior Home Residence and lives there. The daughter, Emily Lewis, is sixteen and there is no record of her in any school or working any job."

"We need to confront this girl and get the truth.

Marvin leaned back in his chair. "I also thought she looked familiar. I think she is the creator of 'Panic' a game much like Tetris. She became famous and then suddenly disappeared from the game scene."

Ron was taking notes. "Do you think she is capable of writing the program 'World Obliteration' for SkyDreams?"

"Absolutely! We need to find her and get the second key."

The General left and headed for the Oval Office to report they had found the designer of 'World Obliteration'. They would be heading back to the Keys. With two days left before the next attack, there was no time to waste. This was their best shot at preventing a worldwide catastrophe.

As they headed from the airport to the Bradley house, there was the sound of a gunshot. The front end started to weave uncontrollably left and right as if a tire had blown out. Other cars did their best to avoid the careening car. Finally the car hit the barrier and headed down a long ravine, rolling over and over. The car came to a stop upside down. No one inside the car was moving.

Chapter Twenty

Emily Lewis had no idea what she had wrought with her program. Despite the daily news about the disasters, she could not bring herself to think that she might have had something to do with it. Besides, there were many computer experts who could shut down the program. And she had been cleared by the authorities who came to her house.

Emily noted it was almost noon and she decided to call her mother and see if they could have lunch together. It was a strange living arrangement with her father somewhere in the deep everglades and her mother living at an assisted living home in exchange for her rehab treatment. She often would visit and have lunch with her mother. Otherwise she lived alone with her royalty checks paying for her expenses. Since she was never enrolled in school no one really knew she existed.

She spent her days creating new games and doing all kinds of research. She would download teaching programs and taught herself math, science, languages, home repairs, and other skills she thought she needed. To protect her location and identity, she created a Faraway cage with Tempest shielding. There was no way she could be located by any device. Finally she took up cooking and created some amazing food combinations which earned her notice on the web.

Emily picked up the phone and called her mother. "Hi mom. It's Emily. I thought I would come over and..."

Rosa sounded out of breath. "Emily, love, I have been called into emergency service. I put myself on volunteer service as an emergency room nurse. I just got a call of a horrible vehicle accident with many casualties. I will call you when I get time. I love you."

The phone went silent. Emily had witnessed this before and she was proud of her mother still being able to help out in an emergency. She originally lost her license due to drinking but she had been sober for the last three years. She could not afford the cost of rehab so she made a deal with the assisted living people. She would be the on-duty nurse in exchange for rehab treatment.

Rosa Lewis arrived at St. Palm Hospital where there was the usual amount of chaos when an accident occurred. She checked in with the charge nurse. "Betty, what have we got?"

"Hi Rosa. It's a bad one. The car was packed with people and it looked like a tire had blown out. They rolled down a ravine landing on the roof. Firemen used the 'jaws of life' and cut them out of the vehicle. We have four males, one of which is a kid, and two females. They were being followed by two military police escorts who thankfully were able to start treatment and call for help."

"Any identifications you want me to do?"

"Not yet. We are still waiting for information on…"

Suddenly a dozen military police and an equal amount of state troopers swept into the emergency room and took up positions around the injured. The area looked like an army camp. "Who is in charge here?"

"I'm Doctor Roman. Please get your men out of here so we can work."

"Sorry doctor, but these individuals are on a critical national mission. Where is General Campbell?"

Doctor Roman checked the charts. "He is in Room C2."

The Captain headed for the General's room. "General, Sir, are you okay?"

Campbell was bandaged from head to toe, an IV in his arm, and two orderlies ready to take him to the operating room. "Captain, get my people out of here as fast as possible. You must find the kid, his name is Marvin, and get him out of here."

Marvin was the lucky one. He was sandwiched between Ron and Ivan who acted like a protective cocoon. Bleeding from cuts to his arms from flying glass, he had no major injuries. The Captain collected him, along with Maddy, who was not badly hurt, and rushed them into a waiting vehicle.

"General Campbell has ordered me to take you to this location."

Marvin was badly shaken. He could not speak coherently and he was faint. His heart beat so hard in his chest he thought it would explode. He kept demanding to know how the others were. "Please, how is everyone? What is going on? Take me back to the hospital!"

Maddy was also groggy but the shot she was given began to take effect and she felt more like herself. "Captain, what is the story with the others?"

"I don't have much information. The General is in surgery for broken bones and internal bleeding. One of the others was found dead at the scene."

Marvin and Maddy both reacted in panic when they heard someone was killed. In unison they both yelled, "Who was killed?"

"Sorry, I do not know. Can you tell me what happened?"

Marvin took a deep breath. "We were on our way to the Bradley house when I heard something like a gunshot. The next thing I knew the car was weaving all over the road, hitting a barrier, and rolled down a hill. As I was trapped between two men I was spared injury."

The Captain picked up the radio. "Command, this is Rescue. Over."

"This is command. Over."

"Witness says a gunshot was heard. Check to see if a front tire was shot out. Over."

"I'll relay the message. Over."

"Any word on the victims? Over."

"All survived except for the one killed at the site. Over."

"Who was it? Over."

"It was a man, no ID yet. Over."

"Keep me up to date. Out."

Marvin and Maddy looked at each other. The victim was either Ron or Ivan. "Maddy, you must think I am a bad person but I hope it was Ivan."

Maddy did not say a word.

Chapter Twenty-One

"NO WAY! I CAN'T DO IT! YOU CAN'T MAKE ME!"

Maddy was trying to calm Marvin down but not having much luck. They were outside the Bradley house and she had discussed a plan that had Marvin front and center. "Marvin, it is the best way, the only way, for us to get that key."

Marvin was just a little calmer. "I'm not good at talking with them."

"Who is them?"

"Girls! She will take everything wrong and laugh at me. Isn't there a computer program that will do it?"

Maddy shook her head. "Listen. We need the key and you are perfect for this plan. You are both sixteen so you must have a lot in common. Surely when you went on a date you were able to make conversation."

He looked at her and had a little frown on his face. She knew his secret. He had never been on a single date with a girl. He was the typical teen male who buried himself in his computer to avoid any social contact. That just wasn't going to work here.

"Marvin, girls are just like boys. What I mean is they have doubts and fears as well. You have plenty in common and you can convince her, with your charm, to stop the program."

"What if I make it worse? She will destroy the other key and the program will continue to kill people."

"We are not going to let that happen. Now, pull yourself together and let's go knock on her door."

A minute later they were standing outside the house. He knocked on the door and took a step back. Emily opened the door and seemed to smile when she saw him. She was dressed in jeans that had more holes than fabric and a sweatshirt with the name of some band spitting fire and blood. Her hair was in a ponytail and her feet were bare. She folded her arms over her chest. "Well, it is nice to see you again, Martin."

"It's Marvin."

"Sorry, I guess I am just a scatterbrain. And you are Maddy?"

"Yes. May we come in?"

"Sure. I like this hunk of a man."

Marvin was now in full panic mode. When he looked at her his body gave him all the proper responses. He knew about girls and social things and hormones and such but he was not sure what to do with it. The first thing he did was trip over the door sill and bump into her. "I'm sorry… really sorry… are you okay? Did I hurt you?"

Emily smiled and laughed. "I'm tough so don't you worry. What are you doing here? I hope you came just to see me."

Maddy stepped between them. "We need your help stopping the computer game you launched called 'World Obliteration'."

"I've never heard of such a game. You must have me confused with someone else."

Marvin finally came alive. "We know you wrote the program for SkyDreams and the program has created its own identity and is carrying out the disasters programmed into it. I have pictures of Guam and O'Hare. Soon North Korea will be destroyed. You have got to help us stop that from happening."

Emily had a terrified look on her face. She staggered a bit as she backed up and dropped into a chair. She shook her head and began to speak in incomplete sentences. "No…it cannot…the code is fictional...there is a failsafe switch. Did you try the failsafe switch?"

"Yes. The AI portion you put in has changed the security program. The failsafe is no longer useable. I worked on it in Beta and I found one of the keys. I am not sure if the keys will still work but we have to try."

"YOU worked on the Beta? Do you even know anything about computer coding? Did they pick you up out of school detention and gave you some kind of deal?"

Marvin was getting angry which gave him more courage. "Look, I'm not here to trade insults or beg. We need to shut down the program or North Korea will disappear!"

She seemed in a trance or daydream. She did not respond to her name or any questions. The idea that her program had caused so much death and destruction caused her to freeze. "I...I...had no idea. How did it happen? I have to look at the code and see what went wrong."

Emily got up and headed for a room off to the side. Marvin followed her and Maddy stayed back. It had to be only the two teens working together. The room had two large monitor screens and a desktop computer with wires running all over the room. The television was attached to it along with an AM radio. The internet was up on one screen and the other appeared to be dark web material. There were three telephone receivers attached to landlines. The room was darkened by heavy duty shades.

"Emily, please, pull up the program and type in your key. I'll type in my key and we will enter them together."

It was as if she were on autopilot. She made the necessary moves and entered the proper commands, and for the first time Marvin could see the entire code. It was beautifully done and looked so simple to him. He typed in his key code and she did the same. All they had to do was hit the enter key at the same time and the program would end, and North Korea would be saved.

"Press…enter…**NOW!**"

They did and the program began to flash several different tabs and links to different sites. There was sound for the first time and photos scrolled across the screen. After fifteen minutes everything stopped. Emily was still staring at the screen and Marvin felt as if a huge weight had been lifted from him. Maddy slowly came into the room. "Has the program halted? Is it stopped?"

Emily had tears in her eyes. Marvin instinctively hugged her.

Chapter Twenty-Two

The room was filled with every technological monitor. There were beeps and a low hum. Numbers flashed across the face of the devices telling the staff what every part of the General's body was doing. The bed was not an ordinary hospital bed but a full-size hybrid with memory foam and a soft topper. Room temperature was set to the General's comfort level and the door was guarded by two MPs.

The surgery was successful and General Campbell lay in the ICU with enough tubes coming out of his body to make him look like a weird science experiment. Pain killers were always appreciated and the General was feeling very relaxed. He looked up expecting to see a nurse or doctor but instead he saw Frank Pierce.

"Frank! Nice to see you. What's the President's favorite Secret Service agent doing here?"

Pierce's face showed no emotion. "I'm glad you are doing better. You have a visitor."

Campbell turned his head and saw President Phillips entering the room. "Mr. President, please forgive me for not standing up."

Whether it was the drugs or the operation, Campbell broke into laughter. "See what I said? Forgive me for not standing up!"

President Phillips smiled. "General, you are an important person to me on a professional and personal level. But one more joke like that and you will be guarding the New Jersey Waste Station."

They both laughed. Phillips came over and took Campbell's hand. "You had us worried for a minute. How are you doing?"

"I'm okay now. They told me I was lucky that the seat belt and air bag cushioned and protected me. One broken leg and bruised ribs I can handle. I appreciate the visit but you didn't come here just to say hello."

"George, I am in a bit of a quandary and I need your guidance."

"Okay, Mr. President, what is the issue?"

Phillips pulled up a chair. "I don't know if they told you that Ivan Kuznetsov was killed in the crash. He was wearing no seat belt and was wedged against the door blocking the air bag. He didn't suffer."

"Yes, the doctor told me. He was a good person and he will be missed."

"The problem is his personal effects. We recovered his cell phone."

Campbell began to put things together. "Despite my high level of pain killers I can see what the problem is. That cell phone will be loaded with all sorts of information that would be important to us. But what will the consequences be if they find out we copied his phone?"

Two nurses came in and when they saw Phillips they did a fast turn around and ran out of the room. "Mr. President, you still have a great impact on the ladies."

"Seriously, George, should we open it or just leave it. The last number he called was to the Kremlin and it is a number we do not have on file. It may be a direct line to Putin."

"Have you asked Ron Faulkner? He's our spy guy."

"He was so anxious to get his hands on the cell that I had to have four MPs stop him."

Campbell shifted in his bed. "I suppose you tried the old 'what would the Russians do' if they had one of our cells."

The phone rang in the ICU, which was not supposed to happen. But when you're a General and a confidant of the President, anything is possible. Campbell picked up the phone. "Yes. Glad to hear it. Yes, do it. I am fine. Time is running out."

"Who was that?"

"Maddy Kraus. She and Marvin found the creator of the game and they are working with her to shut it down."

"Her?"

"Another teenager who is so far ahead of us it hurts."

The nurses came back. "I am sorry, Mr. President, but we have to change dressings and proceed with his sponge bath."

Phillips smiled. "That's my cue to head out of here. You take it easy on that grumpy old man. If he gives you any trouble you call the White House and I will have him deported!"

The nurses looked at each other in horror. "No, please, he is a nice man. Do not send him away!"

Campbell and Phillips both began to laugh. "I'll let you know what I decide."

Phillips returned to the White House and called in the Deputy Chief of NSA, the Director of the CIA, and his Cabinet Secretary of Homeland Security.

"Lady and Gentlemen, you are to break the code on this phone and report its contents to me, personally. Do not mention this to anyone else. And try to preserve the phone so no one else will know you have decrypted it."

The decision had been made. Would the phone give up a treasure or would it be a bust?

Chapter Twenty-Three

Things were not going well at the Bradley house. Both keys had been entered and the program continued to run. The AI had created a third key on its own. Emily and Marvin went line by line but found nothing beyond what they had written. The AI had hidden the new code. It was time to try something 'out of the box'.

Emily's workroom was in the basement, which was unusual as most Florida homes did not have basements. There were no windows, which made the room feel like a prison cell. "Who built this room?"

"That would be my dad. As he got worse and increasingly paranoid, he began to turn the house into a fortified base. He ran electric lines without permits and used double cinderblock walls with concrete and steel in between. There is an air exchanger, and the room is surrounded by a cooling system. He also put in that small elevator so he could bring equipment into the room."

Marvin looked around. "The cement floor must be several feet thick and I imagine you have some kind of pump to remove any water that leaks in. The only other thing I'm curious about is that small cabinet by the back wall."

Emily walked over to it. "This holds two guns along with ammunition and a first aid kit. He used to take me shooting so I would not be afraid to use them. My mother wanted the guns out of the house. They used to fight over it."

He got up and joined her. "When did your father disappear?"

"One night he got up, came down here, went upstairs and walked out the door. That was three years ago. My mom used alcohol to calm her nerves and when that stopped helping, she turned to drugs. There is a house down the street where a drug pusher lives."

Marvin felt both anger and sympathy. "We better get back to the program and see what else we can do."

Maddy came downstairs carrying a tray with food and drinks. "You guys have to keep your strength and health up. Time for lunch although I must warn you I am not the world's best cook."

The three sat beside the server/computer and talked about different times in their lives when things seemed so simple. Maddy's cell rang. She listened intently, said nothing, then hung up. "A little good news. I just got a call from Ron. He is okay and so is the General and his aide. Unfortunately, Ivan was killed."

The news that Ron was okay really lifted Maddy's spirits. Marvin took note of her smile and the fact she was humming. "Well, Maddy, you are happy with the news that Ron is okay. Is there something you want to tell us?"

Maddy smiled. "It's none of your business. Now finish your lunch and let's get back to work."

Emily removed a curtain that was hanging on a wall. Under it was a whiteboard and markers. The board was filled with mathematical equations and some weird drawings. There was also what looked like a love letter drawn up by Gene for his wife Rosa. It asked for forgiveness and expressed his undying love.

Maddy looked at the board. "Without context I can't figure out what this means. I can say that Emily's father really loved both his wife and daughter. He must have been suffering deep emotional pain."

There were tears forming in Emily's eyes. Marvin reached over and gave her a hug. "I'm sure your dad is safe and sound."

Emily brightened up, picked up the marker, and started to list ideas on how to stop the program. According to Marvin's calculations, the next attack was just twenty-four hours away.

She began the long process of trying to stop the program. "First we entered the keys. That did not work as AI created a new lock. It would take too long to try and find it."

Marvin joined her at the board. "And the AI would probably create another new lock."

She continued. "Next we tried detaching the computer from its power supply. But the computer is drawing power from the atmosphere much like a solar cell does. That means unless we create a vacuum it is not a viable approach."

Marvin shook his head. "I have an idea, but it would kill the three of us."

Emily walked over to him. "That sounds ominous. What is it?"

Maddy and Emily sat surrounding Marvin. "In many war games, when the enemy is about to break through the lines, the commander would call in artillery strike on his own location. I have used that several times in my games and it succeeds every time. Unfortunately, my avatar is killed seventy percent of the time."

Emily stood up. "You want to have the computer destroy the computer. And since we are here it would destroy us as well."

"Yes. One of us has to stay here to be sure the plan works. AI might try to stop the plan. Someone has to keep watch."

Maddy was a bit unnerved. "Okay, so we kill one of us to protect the rest of the world. I never saw that coming."

Marvin smiled. "Sort of like looking at the big picture, isn't it? Anyway we cannot open the program to stop it but we don't need a key to change the coordinates of where the next strike will be. Instead of the North Korean coordinates…"

Emily finished the sentence. "…we enter our coordinates."

The three sat in silence. They knew the plan could work but it would take one of them to counterprogram any AI attempt. That means two of them would escape just before the attack and be able to report what happened. Hopefully, they would be able to prevent someone else from repeating the disaster.

"So how do we decide who stays?"

Maddy was first to speak. "It's obvious. I stay because the two of you have a lot of life to live.

Your expertise will help develop other programs that will help mankind. Also, I have no family."

Emily crossed her arms over her chest. "Not going to happen. I created this program and I could not live with the deaths of either one of you. I already have been having nightmares and stress-related ailments over what the machine has already done. It is my fault. Therefore I should stay."

Marvin added his perspective. "Maddy, you run a critical agency that needs to develop into a worldwide safety net. And Emily has shown just how brilliant she is and will make an amazing contribution to the world. I should stay."

Chapter Twenty-Four

It was a case of good news, bad news. The good news was General Campbell was making a faster recovery than expected. The bad news was what was found on Ivan Kuznetsov cell phone.

Now out of the ICU, the General was in a private room with a guard at the door. The room was spacious having a main bedroom and a sitting room. There was plenty of light and the walls were painted a soft green with yellow accents. The bed was not standard issue but came from a special manufacturer. There were computers and large television sets in each room, and a dedicated phone that was connected to the White House. The floors looked like polished marble. The rooms were connected to an HVAC system for a constant hot/cold comfortable temperature.

The General spent most of the time in bed but was able to get up and sit in the recliner in the sitting room. Visitors and staff came in and out so regularly that it appeared the General was back at the

Pentagon. Using a ZOOM-like program, the General was connected to all parts of the military. He had just been appointed as the new Chairman of the Joint Chiefs of Staff.

Ron Faulkner was reading over the transcript of Ivan's cell phone. "George, we have a real problem here. Ivan received a text from the Kremlin telling him a team had been sent to 'neutralize' any attempt to stop the program. They want North Korea to become desperate and come to them for protection."

Campbell took a sip of some water and started to choke. The sound of coughing brought two nurses, two orderlies, a doctor, and men guarding the General to see if the General was in a health emergency. "I'm fine. Get out! All of you!"

Ron reread the last page. "Ivan's orders are to create a safe place for the team to stay. And the team must kidnap the programmer and bring her back to Russia."

"Have you forwarded that information to Maddy and Marvin?"

"Yes. But right now they have a desperate situation."

"What is going on?"

Ron printed out the last contact from Maddy and her group. He handed it to the General who read it in silence. It was all there including the discussion of which one would stay with the program while it self-destructs. The General yelled out a four-letter word. "Why the fancy way of destroying the computer brain? They should grab some C-4 and blow it to pieces!"

Ron let out an audible sigh. "The brain that is working the program is buried underground surrounded by concrete, steel, and a kind of bullet proof vest. The only way to be sure to destroy all of it is by using the power of the computer itself. I just wish there were some other way to control the computer besides sitting next to it."

Campbell got up and limped his way back to bed. Ron followed. "Who built that casing around the AI brain?"

"The room was created by Gene Lewis, father of Emily Lewis, who used to be part of the Army Corps of Engineers. He developed paranoid delusions and so he constructed this impenetrable casing. His friends in the service helped design and build it."

"Is there anything else I should know?"

Ron pulled up a map of Fleming Key in the Florida Keys. "This is where that brain is located.

This area I'm circling in red will be destroyed along with the brain."

The General shook his head. "That's where SFUWO is located along with a large population of citizens."

Ron nodded. "I'm afraid so. We will have to rebuild it."

Campbell yelled and it brought in the MPs. "That's the Special Forces Underwater Operations school where we train divers to work underwater and be ready for submarine rescues. There are a lot of officers from other countries that train there as well."

"But we have enough time to evacuate so there should be no problem."

The General groaned as he moved his body. "The SFUWO school is really just a cover for the secret training of people from other countries to spy for us. If we try to move it, the media will somehow find out and set the spy program back years."

Just then the television monitor popped on. Both men looked up to see the President. "General, I hope you are healing well. What's the latest?"

Neither man knew who should deliver the bad news. After a brief staring match, the General started. "Mr. President, the Russians plan to stop us from destroying the program until after the North Korean site is demolished. They also plan on kidnapping Emily Lewis and Marvin Foster. With Ivan dead, we have no way of finding out who is on the team Russia sent."

"What will happen to Fleming Key?"

Ron took this one. "The Key is only about two miles long and a quarter of a mile wide. There will be little hope of anything surviving. I have already alerted my men to search for the Russians."

Campbell gave the President the odds of success. "We're looking at fifty/ fifty that the AI will not be able to stop us. I sent orders to evacuate the northern end of the Key. With all the chaos we cannot be sure if everyone will get off, and if Ron's men will find the Russians."

The President was hoping for an option. "And there is no other way to destroy that AI brain?"

Campbell shook his head. "We both looked into it. There is one alternative we have not discussed."

"And what is that?"

Ron picked up the thought. "Let the program destroy Punggye-ri and deal with the aftermath."

"Gentlemen, that is not an option. With the evacuation, we will save most of the citizens on

Fleming Key. To let the program run will kill hundreds of thousands of North Koreans. There is an old saying; look at the big picture."

The President signed off. Ron got on his phone and checked in with his men. They had not found anyone who might be part of the Russian team. Meanwhile Campbell was getting updates on the evacuation. With the help of social media, they had planted a false warning of an earthquake with flooding about to hit the area. The computer's explosion would be reported as a gas main blowing up.

Chapter Twenty-Five

William Peter Richards awoke to the sound of his alarm. He hated Mondays but he needed to get going. He rolled over and saw an empty place where his wife, Shelly, normally slept. He figured she was in the kitchen getting the kids' lunches ready and cooking breakfast. He shaved, showered, and dressed quickly before the twins started running around the house.

"Good morning, sweetie. Your husband awakes and is ready to face the day!"

Shelly was busy and did not even look up. "I'm happy for you. Now make sure the twins are dressed and get them down for breakfast."

"Yes, my General. I live to obey your commands."

She looked up and waved the spatula at him. "One of these days I'm going to get duct tape and tape your mouth shut."

Before he could move the twins, Brian and Andrew arrived in all sorts of dress with shirts hanging out and pants slowly sliding for lack of a belt. Richard carried one over his shoulder and the other rode on his foot back to the bedroom. When all was in proper order he took the four-year-old twins back to the kitchen.

The kids rushed to their plates of pancakes and glasses of juice. Richard noticed that his wife was not humming as usual. The small counter television was on and he recognized an old friend, Beth Younis, from his old days in ROTC.

"Sweetie, would you please turn up the sound. That looks like BB from the ROTC."

The voice was that of a reporter for Channel Five news. "I'm talking with Major Younis about the massive evacuation here at the northern tip of Fleming Key. Major, some are asking if the entire Key is in danger or just the northern tip."

"John, let me assure the citizens of the Key that it is only the northern tip. People who live in the central part of the Key will not be affected by the earthquake, really a sea quake, or any flooding. People should take precautions anyway and be sure their pumps are in working order."

William sat down and had a glazed look on his face. He started to talk to the television. "What the hell is going on? There is no possibility of either a quake or a flood. That is garbage. Who the hell made that announcement?"

His wife turned off the sound so as not to upset the children. "Bill, I thought your branch of the military would be aware of what was going on. Why are you surprised by this report?"

"Because we were not made aware of this incident. We may be the Space Force branch of the military but we are supposed to be kept in the loop about anything the military is involved in."

He rushed out the door without kissing anyone and jumped in his car. He took out his cell and called his aide. "Felix, what the hell is with this evacuation for a non-existent earthquake."

"Sorry Bill, I thought it was a drill. It was broadcast on social media and a number of people are trying to chase its origin. We appear to have traced it to the Pentagon but I can't see why they would do something like this."

"Keep up the search while I go see an old friend to find out what is going on."

Meanwhile the northern tip of Fleming Key was emptying out and special protections were in place for SFUWO. Bill, a full Colonel, knew about the secret spy project at the Special Forces site. The appearance of General Campbell's aide, Beth, at the site further proved there was something unusual going on. It would be nice to catch up with Beth, called BB during her ROTC days.

Campbell got a full report and seemed pleased. They had cleared out the area of the program's target and everything was on schedule. Now the decision had to be made about who stayed with the AI brain to keep it distracted while the targeting was complete. It seemed surreal that humans had to hide information from a computer.

"Maddy, are you there? This is General Campbell."

"We are all here. I'm staying and Marvin and Emily will be leaving."

Emily took the mic. "Sorry General, but this Emily is going nowhere. I guess it will be the three of us."

Then Marvin took the mic. "General, if we target the attack out to sea, out of everyone's way, we could buy us more time to figure out how to kill this thing. I know you went to a lot of trouble getting the plan approved, and evacuated the site, but I believe I have another way to accomplish our goal."

Campbell sat up. "If there is even one chance in a thousand, I am willing to risk it. With the tip of the Key empty, we can try your idea and if it does not succeed we can still go back to the original plan."

The General reported the information to the President and everyone was in agreement. Marvin and Emily began work on Marvin's idea. "The AI brain is prepared for every eventuality. What if we take the brain apart, piece by piece, so it will not realize what we are doing?"

Emily nodded. "So we disconnect one wire at a time being careful not to rush things which would tip off the brain."

"Exactly! I'm going to cut the grounding wire. That will not be noticed as it is a piece that the brain does not use."

They looked at their watches. Suddenly Emily leaned forward and kissed Marvin on the cheek. "That's for good luck!"

Wire after wire was cut and the program continued to function. There was no action to prevent the wire cutting. After one hour almost fifty percent of the connections had been cut. As Marvin snipped the main power supply button, he noticed that the timer and the lights were still active.

Marvin put down the cutters. "This is weird. I cut more than half of the connections and the timer has shown no change. Can you run a self-diagnostic to see how the program is running?"

Emily took out a meter. "Absolutely."

Marvin leaned forward and kissed her on the cheek. "That's for good luck."

Emily ran the self-diagnostic and to their surprise there was no damage, no loss of any function. The AI brain had created a false pathway to fool them.

Chapter Twenty-Six

Bill Richards joined the ROTC in college and at his first training exercise he met Beth. After four years training together he thought Beth would be the one. But upon graduation, she went to Command School while he joined NASA. Now she was General Campbell's aide while he was second in command of the new Space Force division. As he drove, he thought about what to say when he saw Beth. They had lost touch fifteen years ago and now he was married with twins. He wondered if she had ever married.

His military uniform and ID got him past all the roadblocks. He arrived at the temporary command tent, brushed his uniform, and straightened his tunic to make a good impression. He entered the tent and a sentry stopped him. "Colonel, sir, how may I help you?"

"I would like to speak with Major Younis."

"I'm sorry sir but the Major is not taking any visitors. I suggest you leave your information and someone will get back to you."

"Sergeant, I am Colonel Richards with the Space Force and I need to speak with Major Younis. And I mean now!"

Given the loud command, the sentry was joined by two additional MPs. "As I said, the Major cannot be disturbed."

Beth heard the commotion and entered the room. She saw Bill and it caught her by surprise. He looked just as handsome as he was all those years ago. He was one part of her life she thought she had buried deep in her mind. The romantic memories came flooding back ending with the day they said goodbye.

She snapped out of the daydream. "Colonel William Richards, friend and lover."

"Major Bethany Younis, the one who got away."

The guards slowly backed away. Beth walked over to him, wrapped her arms around his body, and kissed him on the cheek. "It is so good to see you again. I really miss our time together. How have you been?"

Bill looked back at the sentry who slowly walked out of the tent. "Beth, you are even prettier today than you were so many years ago."

She let go of him. "Are you here to renew old times or is this business?"

"I think a little of both. But first the business of what is happening here on the Key. What's this baloney about an earthquake? And why wasn't my command notified?"

Beth slipped her arm under his arm and led him into her office. They both sat for just a moment burning to ask so many questions. But first to business.

"Bill, what is going on is top secret at the highest levels. The President himself is running this. I'm not sure what I can tell you at this point."

He smiled. "You can't tell me because the operation is a 'need to know' and what you are doing here is a black op."

Beth was caught between her feelings for him, her desire to include a valuable asset, and protocol. She thought about calling General Campbell for guidance. "Bill, what I am about to tell you can never leave this room."

"Beth, you can trust me. I just want to know what the danger is to the U. S. and if I can help."

For the next hour Beth filled him in down to the smallest detail. She could not tell if the look on his face was one of shock or surprise.

"That is a lot to take in. What have you tried to stop the program? How much do you think Russia knows? Are there any other players in this game?"

Beth outlined all the attempts and revealed the information that came from Ivan's phone. "Our last attempt was to snip wires, but the brain detected it and just led us on a wild goose chase."

Bill sat deep in thought. Beth worried she might have gone too far. She almost thought she could see his brain turning and planning. "You did not mention if you tried either an EMP or GMD?"

Beth shook her head. "I think so. I'll call Marvin and ask."

She picked up her radio and called Maddy and the teens. "Ask Emily and Marvin about using an EMP or GMD pulse."

Maddy looked at the teens. "Beth wants to know if you have tried either an EMP or GMD pulse."

It was as if a light went off inside Emily's head. "Of course, that could do it. There is no shielding against either of those around the program. I think we have done it!"

Marvin shook his head. "Sorry, I had thought of that but we cannot generate a pulse strong enough to affect the program."

Beth relayed the information to Bill. "Sorry, they tried it but not enough power behind the pulse."

"That's strange. The pulse we generate will knock out an entire country."

"Marvin did you hear that. Colonel Richards says you should be able to have enough power to do the work."

"Tell the Colonel we used the most powerful pulse on earth."

Bill picked up the phone. "Who said I was talking about a pulse generated from earth?"

He pushed the speaker phone button so they could all talk and hear. "Colonel, what are you talking about?"

Bill put his head in his hands. "I just leaked highly classified information. What I am about to tell you can never leave this area. I will deny I ever said it and you will all be in prison. Along with me."

Beth put her hand on his shoulder. "You can trust us. I trusted you."

Bill slowly gave up the secret. "We have a satellite that has a directed beam of EMP energy far stronger than anything on earth. It just might work."

Emily looked at Marvin. "What is EMP and GMD?"

Marvin smiled. "Electromagnetic Pulse and Geomagnetic Disturbance and the answer to our prayers!!"

Chapter Twenty-Seven

Beth smiled. "We need some time to catch up."

Bill nodded. "It would be great but right now I need to get to the location of the main computer core."

Beth agreed. "Business before pleasure, especially if that business is to stop the destruction of the world."

Beth gave Bill the location. "Bill, be careful. We have discovered there is a Russian assassination team here to make sure the program runs, and to kidnap Emily and Marvin."

"Don't worry, my intense smile will disarm them!"

"Always with the jokes. There are two soldiers by the entryway to the next tent. I'll order them to provide you with an escort."

Beth and Bill walked out and Beth turned to the two soldiers standing in the next entryway. "You men. You are to escort Colonel Richards to an address he will give you."

Neither of the soldiers responded. Beth gave the order a second time and only one man made any kind of acceptance of the order by saluting. "Bill, I don't know what is with this new generation of soldiers. Good luck. Keep me informed."

Bill headed off with the two soldiers and arrived at the Bradley house. They went inside and down to the basement. There, sitting next to the computer, Emily and Marvin were still discussing who would stay and who would leave. Maddy approached Bill.

"Beth told me about your idea. Is there anything I can do to help?"

Bill shook his head. "I just have to enter the coordinates and codes to make the satellite active."

Marvin got up and slowly walked over to Maddy. "Can I talk to you in private?"

"Of course. Is this about who stays and who goes?"

Marvin looked down at his shoes. "No. There is something wrong with the soldiers. They are wearing combat fatigues but there are no name patches on the tunics."

Maddy turned slowly and saw the blank space where the name should be attached. In addition she noticed one had a Captain's Insignia on one shoulder and a Sergeant's on the other. She walked slowly to her purse and pulled out a gun.

There was a loud explosion as a pistol was fired. Maddy lay on the floor with a wound to her chest. Emily rushed over to try to stop the bleeding. Marvin rushed to the radio to warn others but was hit on the head by the pistol. The other man was restraining Bill.

Bill shouted. **"Who the hell are you and what do you want?"**

"We want you to change the coordinates back to North Korea."

Marvin woke and struggled to get into a sitting position. "*What* do you want?"

"As I just told your commander, I want you to replace the coordinates you have with these."

Marvin looked at the numbers. "This will aim the attack back at North Korea. I will not do that."

Emily cried out. "We need a doctor! Maddy is bleeding and I cannot stop it."

The Russian leader waved his pistol. "If you do not do as I ask I will start shooting everyone. I will start with this soldier."

Marvin tried to push past one guard and grab the second. He was no match for the soldier and Bill was looking into the barrel of a Russian pistol. "Marvin, calm down. I will set the coordinates. Just like you showed me."

The hostage taker nodded. "You are very wise for an American. Now get to work!"

Marvin wanted to stop Bill but he could not. Emily was pressing a jacket onto Maddy's wounds. Bill was working on a side panel of a remote device.

The leader put the gun to Bill's head. "What are you doing? Why are you using that remote panel?"

Bill kneeled down. "The regular panel has been shorted. This remote panel takes its place. The dials should be starting to light up. See, it's working. We better get to cover as this thing **might explode!**"

The two-man team's leader shook his head. "There should be no danger here! All the force with be in North Korea!"

Bill shook his head as he ran to a wall for cover and yelled to Marvin. "The satellite will be in range in five…four…three…two…one!!"

It was like a silent movie. People moving about without saying a word. The hostage takers had no clue about what was happening. The computer brain started to show signs of building up but suddenly it went dark. Bill looked at his digital watch and it had stopped working. The EMP pulse shut down the computer and every electronic device inside the house. The beam had been so precise there was no effect outside the building. And the computer was dark.

"**What did you do**? Get the computer back online! **Now!!**"

The quiet of the room was interrupted by cries coming from Maddy. Emily's hand and wrist were covered in blood. Maddy's breathing was shallow and then it stopped. Emily yelled at Maddy. "**Wake up! Wake up! Please don't die!**"

Bill slid over to Maddy and checked her pulse. "I'm afraid she's dead."

The leader of the team grabbed Marvin. "Okay, you will come with us. We have a boat waiting. Now get up or I will start shooting!"

Bill stood up. "You aren't going to shoot us. Your masters want us alive. We aren't going anywhere!"

The leader aimed his pistol at Bill's head. His hand began to waver. He put the gun down and took out a knife and approached Bill. "I will carve you like a dead pig."

Marvin rushed the man and knocked him to the ground. The second soldier grabbed Emily and put a knife to her throat. "Comply or I will slit her throat!"

Just then two jeeps pulled up to the house. Six soldiers got out and surrounded the building. Major Younis walked up to the front door. "Bill, what happened? Did it work? There has been no destruction at the tip of the Key. Are you all right?"

One of the Russians came to the door holding Emily with a knife to her throat. "Get back. We will take the jeeps. If you try to stop us we will kill them all."

The man holding Emily slowly backed into the building. Beth was not sure what was going on inside but she directed the men to arm their weapons. She yelled into the house. "Surrender your weapons. If we have to come in to get you I cannot guarantee your safety."

One of the assassins yelled back. "And we cannot guarantee you will find the last three hostages alive!"

The threat was expected but the warning only mentioned three hostages. Beth realized someone had already been killed. "Okay, we are backing off. Are all hostages okay?"

"One person tried to be a hero. But everyone else is alive, for now! Get away from the jeeps. You have one minute."

It was going to be a standoff. Since there was no explosion at the tip of the Key it was safe to assume the EMP worked. But now they had to figure a way to get the others out safely.

Chapter Twenty-Eight

Against the doctor's orders, General Campbell was on a flight to Fleming Key. Word had reached him about the Maddy's death and the hostage situation. And he had informed Ron who took it very hard. Ron decided to go back to the office and work from there tracing the background of the two assassins. Citizens were allowed back into their houses with the announcement that the earthquake warning was disinformation spread by someone on the internet.

The General landed at the air station on Fleming Key. Waiting for him was Lars Arvidson, the Russian spy who was also a direct contact to Putin. Lars changed loyalty as often as rain spoiled a picnic. With the threat to North Korea now gone, Campbell hoped he could persuade Putin to call off his assassins.

Lars and Campbell arrived at the Bradley house. They moved into a command tent that had been set up by the Florida State Police. Beth filled them in. "There has been no movement for the last two hours. They made demands but they have not followed up on them. It has been eerily quiet."

The commander of the SWAT team added his information. "According to our scan there are five people alive. Two would have to be the kids, two would have to be the Russians, and that leaves one who we know nothing about."

Beth identified the last one. "His name is Bill Richards and he is a Colonel attached to the Space Force unit. It was his work on a satellite beam that has crippled the AI program. What his condition is we do not know."

Campbell picked up the secure communications line. "Mr. President, I have confirmed that the computer program is no longer a threat. There are two Russian operatives holding three hostages. One of the hostages is Colonel Richards of the Space Force. We assume the children are okay as they are the target of the Russians."

"General, I will speak to the Russians. I'll get back to you."

Meanwhile, Ron Faulkner arrived at the Bradley house. Everyone was staring at him wondering what was going on in his mind. No one was sure what the status of his relationship with Maddy had been, but they knew he was hurting.

"General, I have the background information on the two Russians. They are both special forces and will not give up easily. Lars, what are you doing here?"

"I am trying to help. I am sorry about Maddy."

"So am I. But right now our focus has to be on the hostages. I thought I saw the President on the monitor when I walked in."

Campbell extended his hand to Ron who refused it. "Yes, Lars is going to help us make contact with a high-level minister in Putin's cabinet."

The assassins were calling Beth on the video phone that she had given them. "Major, we are ready to make a deal. We will release Richards and take Emily and Marvin with us as a guarantee you will not try shoot us. When we board our plane we will release them. You have thirty minutes to agree."

Ron was the first to speak. "No way. They are killers. They will kill the teens as soon as they feel safe. We cannot let them get away with murder."

Campbell put his arm on Ron's shoulder. "I understand how you feel. But our main goal here is to get Emily and Marvin back. We can follow them to the air station and set up a trap. If we think it will work, we will spring it. But you have to know that they just might escape."

Ron pushed Campbell's hand off his shoulder. "I never thought I would see you get down on your knees and beg!!"

Beth was angry. "Ron, that is an awful thing to say. The General has always been on your side. I'm sorry about Maddy but we have to think of the lives of the others."

Ron looked outraged. "You both are bending over and kissing their…."

"Ron, that's enough. I think you should leave now so you can get your composure back.'

Ron backed out of the command tent and disappeared.

Chapter Twenty-Nine

He sat alone, nursing his drink, whiskey neat. The bartender would come by every so often to ask if he wanted something more. He shook his head and waved the bartender off. He looked around and there were only two other people in the establishment. One was dirty looking, hair a mess, torn clothes, and mud-covered shoes. The other was a man, one lit cigarette in his mouth and one burning in a makeshift ashtray. The bartender had already told him to stop smoking inside.

Ron got up slowly and moved over to a booth. He sat with his back to the wall and his legs up on the bench seat. He still had his drink but every time he looked at it he would see Maddy's face. Once he thought she was sitting opposite him. She looked so real. The bartender came over once again. "What? Do you need the booth? I paid for my drink."

He looked around. Here in the Keys they did not have bars, they only had taverns. The place was decorated with a sea motif, no surprise there, with pictures of sailboats, motorboats, yachts, and tall ships. There were pieces of sailboat rigging, like ropes, block and tackle, and fake gauges scattered around the floor.

He swiveled and put his head in his hands with his elbows resting on the table. He knew he had to snap out of it but he really did not know how. The door opened and extra sunlight filled the dark room. The next thing he heard was someone calling his name. He slowly looked up. It was his aide, Frank, carrying a large dark black case.

Frank was dressed in a suit and tie rather than a uniform. He put the case on the table. "Mr. Director, I have what you asked for although I am not sure why you wanted it."

Ron looked up. "Frank, are you my aide?"

"Yes, sir."

"And do you take orders from me?"

"Again, yes, sir."

"Do I have to explain myself to you?"

"Yes…I mean no, sir."

"Good. Now leave the case and go back to the Command Center. Tell no one that you saw me and especially not what you brought me. Do I make myself clear!"

"Yes sir. In case you were wondering they have agreed to let the Russians get to the airport where they will have a trap ready for them."

"Thank you. Now go away."

Frank left, and Ron moved the case in front of him. He slowly opened one lock and then the other. He took a gulp of his drink. He lifted the cover and there it sat, shiny and deep black, in separate pieces he would have to assemble. He leaned back and thought about the weapon in the case. He was out hunting and a fellow hunter showed him the AR500 from Big Horn Armory. It took a .500 round that was so powerful it could pass through an engine block. Given the notoriety of AR (Armalite Rifle) rifles, he knew he had to be very careful not to be seen with it.

Ron left the tavern and went into his motel room. He made sure all the blinds were down. He took out the pieces and put them together. Each time he locked in a piece his anger grew. He knew what he was going to do and no one had better stand in his way. He loaded the magazine. He would be heading back to the Bradley house.

Meanwhile at the Command Center, General Campbell and Major Younis had drawn up a plan to capture the Russians and free the hostages. They were still waiting on a call from Russia for permission to terminate the Russian special forces men if that was the only way to free the hostages. An armored truck was waiting by the house to take the Russians and the hostages to the air base. There, on a long gangway to the airplane, agents would be secreted inside false panels and when the group walked by, the agents would push out the false walls and grab the Russians.

"General, there is an incoming message from Lars."

"Yes, Lars, what is the word."

Lars appeared on the computer screen. "General, you have to understand the delicate matter you have created. That computer program must never be allowed to be set up again. Our intention is to merely isolate the designers and bring no harm to them. This way everyone comes out a winner."

Campbell looked over at Beth. "I'm sorry, Lars but I think we can isolate the designers and keep a closer watch on them here in the U.S.. I hope you understand that we will do everything in our power not to harm your men but there are no guarantees."

Lars sounded like he was begging. "George, please, do not do this. I have received orders from

President Putin himself not to allow the designers to remain in your hands. We both agree that killing our men would be a massive setback in our relations. I may not be able to help you anymore in the future."

"Lars, we appreciate what you are saying and we will do our best to put your men on a plane and send them back to Moscow. But we must keep the designers and do whatever it takes to accomplish that."

Lars leaned closer to the camera. "Goodbye, my old friend."

The screen went blank. Campbell realized that Lars's failure might mean his disappearance from the Russian political system. But time was up and the long-awaited movement to the air base was about to begin. The passageway from the terminal to the airplane's door was lined with false walls, hiding the agents. All was set to go.

As the Russians and their hostages moved out of the doorway of the Bradley house all eyes were on them. Emily, Marvin, and Bill were directly in front forming a human shield. They slowly walked to the rear of the armored van. No one noticed the lone figure on the roof of the house directly across the street.

Chapter Thirty

Step One: Find a flat surface that is mostly hidden from view. Done.

Step Two: Open the weapon's case and start to assemble the AR500. Done.

Step Three: Once the barrel is locked, pull out the extended butt. Done.

Step Four: Attach telescopic sight. Done.

Step Five: Lower front legs for stability. Done.

Step Six: Insert magazine. Done.

Step Seven: Scope out the sight. Done.

Step One: Wait for hostages and Russians to come out. Major Younis plays the recording of Lars Arvidson's telephone threat about killing their soldiers. *"We both agree that killing our men would be a massive setback in our relations."* This convinces the Russians to come outside.

Step Two: Calculate the distance and best time to fire.

Step Three: The armored car rear door is opened allowing one of the Russians to get inside leaving the other outside. This will allow Ron to pick off one of the men and give the hostages a chance to duck for cover.

Step Four: Fire rapidly into the armored car until the second Russian is dead.

Step Five: Use the planned escape route. Get into the car and rush to the scene as if he has just arrived.

So it was all planned and the scenario was in motion. The Russians did emerge from the house after hearing Lars's message. The hostages looked much more relaxed and they moved to the rear of the armored car. And as predicted, one Russian entered the car while the other pushed the hostages to the door. Major Younis and her men had moved back to give them plenty of room. All guns had been lowered. With the trap set at the air station, there was no need to rush things.

Ron readied the rifle. He picked out the Russian. He slowly squeezed the trigger. There was a load explosive noise. The bullet hit the hostage taker in the forehead making a half inch hole as the bullet travelled through his head and out the back. The hostages fell to the ground and Beth and her men began a sweep of the scene to locate the shooter.

Several more rounds were fired and each penetrated the armored car's side. Two found their target and the other hostage taker fell out of the vehicle and onto the street. By now one soldier had identified the location of the shooter and opened fire. Several others joined in and multiple bullets went screaming through the air at the roof top.

Ron was already gone. He slid along the roof and got to the portable fire escape ladder he had brought with him. He quickly threw his gun into the trunk and took off figuring he could come around and act as if he had just arrived. But like all plans there was usually a speed bump in the completion. There was a school crossing guard standing and waiting for the noon release of the children. As Ron sped by, the crossing guard got the license plate number and when police arrived he gave it to them.

Beth, amidst the chaos of the shooting scene, called Campbell. "Both Russians are dead but the hostages are okay. We got the license plate of the assassin but I think the numbers might not be in the right order."

"Damn!"

One of the police officers ran the plate. "The plate comes back to Ron Faulkner."

There was silence and then Campbell gave the only order he could. "Find and detain Faulkner. Broadcast an 'armed and dangerous' notice and that he is wanted in connection to two shootings."

Beth was not sure about that, but she had her orders. Given the number of MPs and police from other agencies, the odds of Ron's escaping were about the same as winning a Mega Millions lottery. Just half a mile from the site Ron's car was boxed in by police vehicles. Ron surrendered and opened the trunk. The officers took the gun and placed Ron under arrest.

Beth relayed the news to Campbell. "We caught Ron and he had the rifle with him. There is no doubt he was the shooter. He is being taken to the Air Station jail. I cannot believe it. I cannot believe he would do this."

"Major, I will be arriving shortly. Hold off any interrogation until I arrive. In the meantime, how are the hostages holding up? Were any of them hurt?"

"All is good with them. We were finally able to get to Maddy's body. The kids will be having nightmares for a long time."

Campbell felt some relief. "What about Colonel Richards?"

"He is on his way to check in with his family. He will meet us at the jail."

Campbell was worrying about how the Russians would take the shootings. "And is the AI brain dead? Is it over?"

Beth looked at Marvin. "Is it dead?"

Marvin nodded. "It's fried."

Now all they had to do was contact the Russians and permanently destroy the computer program. They still had no idea why Ron went on the rampage.

Chapter Thirty-One

General Campbell and Major Younis sat quietly, about to witness a most disturbing sight. Ron Faulkner, a long-time partner in many critical government situations, was about to be brought in wearing a bright orange jumpsuit with a number printed on the chest. On the back would be the letters DOC (Department of Corrections). The room was bare with no windows, a table, and four chairs. The two were unsure what would happen when they were face to face with him.

Ron entered with handcuffs and leg cuffs all linked together by a chain around his waist. He looked pale and gaunt. He shuffled over to a chair and sat opposite his former colleagues. They looked at one another and no one was sure who should start. Finally Campbell asked the question that a large number of people wanted to ask. "Why?"

Ron answered in a low voice. "What do you mean why? I had no choice. Those murderers were going back to Russia and would receive a state welcome. They killed my Maddy. They shot my beloved Maddy. They were not going to get away."

Beth reached out to touch him but the guard blocked her hand. "Sorry. Ron, I am so broken up by what happened. I had no idea that you and Maddy were so close."

He looked over at her. "It was only three weeks but we drew closer and closer as tensions grew. We kept everything quiet due to the mission, but I felt there was a future ahead for us. I could tell she felt the same way."

Campbell got right to the consequences of the shootings. "Ron, you will be tried and convicted, given the evidence they have, plus your full confession. You are looking at life with no parole in State court and the possible death penalty in Federal court. We have hired the best criminal attorney we could find. Perhaps the prosecution will offer a deal given the circumstances."

Ron smiled. "I have been in the spy business long enough to learn a few tricks. I do have an idea and I'm hoping you will bring it to the President and advocate for it."

"Sure, anything at all. How about a file in a cake?"

The tension lessened a bit as all three grinned. The guard did not grin, however. "Okay, what is this master plan of yours."

Ron leaned forward as if he was making sure others were not able to hear him. "The two Special Forces soldiers have connections to important people in Russia. Andrei Novikov is the son of Dimitri Novikov who is the chair of the council that advises Putin. His support gave Putin the go ahead to invade Ukraine."

"No wonder the Russians are in a fit."

"Boris Petrov is the son of one of the wealthiest oil ministers in the world. He, like Dimitri, are the foundation of support for Putin."

Campbell was taking notes. "Okay, now we know why the Russians warned us about killing them and why my contact is not answering my calls."

Beth had the next question. "What has this to do with your situation?"

"Simple. The Russians are holding two American journalists and one American contractor on trumped up charges. It would seem that Putin would be willing to make a prisoner exchange: me for the three being held in Russia."

Everything went quiet. Campbell looked at Beth and then back to Ron. Beth had a look of horror on her face. "Ron, no…no…no. The Russians will shoot you as you get off the plane. At least here you would have a chance to live out the rest of your life."

Ron tried to reach out to Beth but could not. "Beth, with Maddy gone and a double murder charge I am not going to have anything to live for. At least this way the Russians will feel we have made amends and they can do anything they want to me. I assume it will not be a simple bullet or drink of poison."

Campbell finally weighed in. "Do you realize what you are doing? The hell with the Russians! Things will eventually calm down. There have been other issues in the past and we got through all of them."

Ron shook his head. "You don't understand. I need to do this. I have taken two lives out of anger and grief. I have disobeyed a direct order from the President. I have failed my country. Let me have this one thing so I can die in peace."

The guard walked over to the table. "I'm sorry, but your time is up."

Beth tried to hug Ron but the guard intervened. Campbell stood up, snapped to attention, and saluted Ron. The guard nodded and then slowly led Ron away.

General Campbell was waiting inside the oval office at the White House. Beth was there along with the Secretary of State, the Secretary of Homeland Security, and Vice-President Susan Mason. When the President entered, they all stood.

President Phillips sat down and went straight to it. "General, I have read your report and I must say I have never been in this position before. Prisoner exchanges are difficult at best but here you have an American wanting to be sent to Russia, most likely to his death."

Campbell addressed the group. "Yes, sir. Ron Faulkner lived his life by a code of honor and served our country for over twenty years since he enlisted at eighteen. He believes this action will accomplish a number of positive outcomes. First, we get back the three prisoners the Russians are holding. Second, we calm the waters for Putin which will help us in the future. And lastly, it gives Ron a way to pay for what he did which will bring him peace."

Vice-President Mason looked over the proposal. "Are we sure Putin will agree to this? And

I have a lot of sympathy for Ron, but we are allowing an American to commit suicide."

Beth, her voice was cracking with every word. "I may be speaking out of turn but Ron is making a great sacrifice, much like volunteers in combat who risk their lives for others. This is no different than a Seal Team going in to free hostages."

There were comments and suggestions from the rest of the group. Both Campbell and Beth were saying silent prayers to let the exchange go through. Finally the discussion ended. President Phillips looked at Campbell. "This is a solid plan. Get the ball rolling on the exchange. As my new Chief of the Joint Chiefs of Staff I like your openness and Major Younis has acquitted herself well. Now if you excuse me I have a meeting to chair."

The President left the room. The Secretary of State shook Campbell's hand and invited him to be part of the negotiations.

Chapter Thirty-Two

They called it a 'mental health' day although it lasted for almost a week. Things seemed to be getting back to normal. General Campbell had been summoned to the Oval Office while Major Younis was finishing sending thank you cards to those who attended Maddy's funeral. Colonel Richards gave his young family extra hugs. Marvin was home but was worried about Emily. The authorities now knew she was living alone without a parent or guardian present.

Campbell entered the office and saw both President Phillips and Vice-President Mason sitting in the center of the room. There were no aides present, which was very unusual. He saluted and waited for the President to invite him to sit.

"Ah, General, please take a seat. You know the Vice-President?"

"Yes, sir. We have worked on a number of projects."

The President took off his reading glasses. "George, you are one of the first people to know this and it is for this room only. I am entering the last year of my Presidency and the party is looking for someone to keep the White House in their column. I plan to endorse the Vice-President, Susan, to lead the campaign."

Campbell looked over at Susan. "My congratulations. The country will be well cared for with you at the helm."

Susan turned to Campbell. "General, you are approaching retirement age from the military and you have reached the highest level in your long and successful career. I would like you to consider retiring now and joining me on the ticket as my Vice-President."

Campbell was stunned. He had never considered the political side of service. He wanted to be a soldier since he was six or seven. He knew very little about campaigning and just what he would do as Vice-President."

President Phillips stood up and offered his hand to the General. "George, you have served this nation brilliantly and with your reputation, your contacts, your damn good common sense, I am sure Susan and the nation will benefit. But it is a big commitment. You should take the time to really think on it."

Susan extended her hand. "General, I hope you will accept. I have set up a meeting for the two of us next week. I know it is sexist to mention it, but the voters will feel better if I have a strong male at my back."

Campbell shook hands. "Madam Vice-President, you do not need me to show the voters what a solid and knowledgeable leader you are."

Campbell's mind was running all sorts of scenarios as he sat at his desk in the Pentagon. He had never considered himself to be someone people would vote for. His daydream was interrupted by the intercom announcing that Major Younis had arrived. He buzzed her in.

"Ah, 'Colonel Younis', how did your 'mental health' day work out? We have been through quite a lot and I know Maddy's death was a hard blow for you."

Beth sat down next to the General's desk. "I did some reflection and some praying. Maddy's funeral was exceptional with a full military honor guard. But at this point I am still a little worried about you. You addressed me as Colonel."

Campbell had a sheepish grin on his face. "That was no error, Colonel. You better update your uniform. Congratulations!!"

Beth did not know what to say. She wanted to jump up and down and shout as loud as she could but all that came out of her mouth was a thank you. "I am happy to continue as your aide, General. I think we work very well together."

She was not prepared for what Campbell said next. "Colonel, I'm afraid that will not be possible. I will be retiring from the military to take on a different challenge. I will offer you your choice of new assignment. Where in the military would you like to serve?"

Beth thought for a moment when something suddenly hit her. "I worked very closely with Ron Faulkner and helped him on a number of cases. I met most of his contacts around the world and he was really my mentor. I would like to replace him at the NSA."

"Good choice! I approve and will set the wheels in motion."

Beth looked puzzled. "That appointment is up to the President. You will have to get it cleared by him."

The General laughed. "I do not believe that will be a problem."

"Have you any news about Ron?"

Campbell's face gave away the news. "I'm sorry to tell you that as soon as Ron arrived in Russia he disappeared. We have no idea where he is or what happened to him. The three Americans we got back are with their families."

Just then the intercom buzzed and the aide announced that Marvin Foster and his family, along with Emily Lewis and her mother, had arrived. The General buzzed them in.

Both Marvin and Emily were surprised to see Beth and rushed over to greet her. "Major, it is so nice to see you."

"Sorry. But it is not Major anymore. You can call me Colonel Younis."

Marvin and Emily gave her a hug. The General walked over and greeted the families. "Please, won't you all sit down. I have something to discuss with all of you."

Emily and Marvin sat side by side holding hands but with their parents around they quickly put their hands on their laps. Marvin's dad, John, tried to make conversation talking about the size of the Pentagon. Mary Foster, Marvin's sister, looked around and slowly put her cell phone away. Emily's mother, Rosa, kept rubbing her hands together.

The General leaned on his desk facing everyone. "It is no secret that the help Marvin and Emily provided saved the world from the most dangerous situation since the old Cold War. Even though Emily's program got out of control, it has become a key lesson on deciding what to do with AI. You should be very proud of your children and what an amazing gift they are."

John Foster stood up. "Thank you General. We are indeed very proud of Marvin, and Emily whom we just met."

"Your children are unique and a valuable resource for the nation. Therefore, I have done some maneuvering and found both Marvin and Emily a place where they can continue to grow into special people. My brother is the Director of Admissions at M. I. T. in Boston. He has set up a special program for the two geniuses and has enrolled them in a degree granting program. This will be with all expenses paid."

The room was silent. Marvin and Emily looked at each other and their facial expressions just grew happier and happier. They looked at their parents and saw their heads nodding up and down. All of a sudden Marvin jumped up and yelled **YES**! Everyone broke out in laughter and there were hugs all around. Campbell picked up his phone and called his aide. "Take these people to the cafeteria. There is a large buffet for lunch and of course there is a lot of cake and ice cream."

The group left still talking about the opportunity the teens had been given. Campbell and Younis held back for one more guest who had just arrived. "Colonel Richards, please come in."

"General, Major, it is a pleasure to see how well it all turned out."

Beth enjoyed correcting everyone. "Colonel, I am no longer a Major. I have climbed the ranks and am now a Colonel."

Richards extended his hand. "Well deserved. I guess we can sit at the same table in the Officer's lounge."

Campbell laughed. "I'm afraid that will not be possible. Colonel Richards, you are now General Richards and sole commander of the Space Force Division of the Military. Congratulations!"

Richards' expression was one of both disbelief and total excitement. "Thank you General. And you too, Colonel."

"Okay, now that everything is done, there is some great food awaiting us in the cafeteria. As a high ranking general I declare it is legal to start with the cake and ice cream first."